Wings of Gold

Robert F. Dorr and Robert D. Ketchell

Motorbooks International
Publishers & Wholesalers

First published in 1990 by Motorbooks International Publishers & Wholesalers, P O Box 2, 729 Prospect Avenue, Osceola, WI 54020 USA

Motorbooks International books are also available at discounts in bulk quantity for industrial or sales-promotional use. For details write to Special Sales Manager at the Publisher's address

Library of Congress Cataloging-in-Publication Data
Dorr, Robert F.
    Wings of gold/Robert F. Dorr, Robert D. Ketchell.
        p.   cm.
    ISBN 0-87938-439-5
    1. United States. Navy—Aviation.   2. United States.
Navy—Vocational guidance.   3. Aeronautics, Military—
United States—Vocational guidance.   4. Air pilots,
Military—United States.
    I. Ketchell, Robert D.   II. Title.
VG93.D67 1990   90-35073
359.9′4′02373—dc20   CIP

Printed and bound in Hong Kong

On the front cover: Student and instructor return to the ready room after an instruction flight in a TA-4 Skyhawk. *Rob Ketchell*

On the back cover: A student pilot preflights a T-2 Buckeye before a solo training hop. *Rob Ketchell*

On the frontispiece: A student naval aviator brings a T-2C Buckeye in to land on the boat. *USN*

On the title page: Two Buckeyes pay tribute to a graduating class. *Rob Ketchell*

On the verso page: A student rockets skyward after a touch and go. *Rob Ketchell*

Contents

The Goal...

...The First
Step

Chapter 1

The Big Picture

To many, US naval aviation means Tom Cruise in *Top Gun*, returning in triumph to his carrier deck in a howling F-14 Tomcat after shooting down hostile MiGs.

In real life, only a few naval aviators live in the world of the Tomcat, made glamorous by Hollywood, or the A-6 Intruder, glorified in a best-selling novel and movie *Flight of the Intruder*. The US Naval Air Training Command prepares men and women to fly no fewer than twenty-four aircraft types, including flying machines as disparate as the RH-53D Sea Stallion helicopter and the C-130 Hercules transport.

Furthermore, for every "maverick" there must be a "goose." The back-seater in *Top Gun*, a naval flight officer (NFO), was as vital to the MiG killing mission as the guy sitting up front. Real NFOs are trained for one of five missions—radar intercept officer (RIO), airborne tactical data systems officer (ATDS) or one of three categories of navigator. Because an NFO really is as important as a pilot—maybe more—he or she goes through equally rigorous training. In addition, the NFO is almost as likely as a pilot to rise to command a squadron or an Air Wing.

This volume will focus on those who fly for the Navy, including wearers of the Marine Corps uniform. Marine pilots are naval aviators every bit as much as their counterparts in the Fleet. It should also be noted

that the Coast Guard annually sends seventy officers through Navy flight training to produce sixty naval aviators. Coast Guard students follow a special program which exposes them to both helicopter and multi-engine flying, and some thirty Coast Guard officers are trained to be flight instructors in the Navy's training program.

Training naval aviators and NFOs is the job of a massive organization, spread around the United States—employing tens of thousands, using no fewer than seven aircraft types in six training wings with twenty squadrons and guiding future aviators down no fewer than nine "pipelines" or paths to gold wings and a flying career—three for pilots, six for NFOs.

A three-star vice admiral with a distinguished background in naval aviation always occupies the job of Chief, Naval Education and Training (CNET) at NAS Pensacola, Florida. Under him, the six wings which instruct pilots and NFOs report to a rear admiral who is Chief, Naval Aviation Training (CNATRA, inevitably pronounced Sinatra), at NAS Corpus Christi, Texas.

Trying to figure out how the system works is vexing even for those in the middle of it. For our overview of naval air training, we'll simplify things by looking at just two future naval fliers and following them on two of those nine pathways towards wings of gold. These are real people with real names: Beth Murray and Joe Fives.

Women, it need scarcely be pointed out, have qualified for naval aviator status ever since LT Barbara Ann Allen became the first in 1973. Female avia-

previous page
This photo montage by Beech Aircraft says it all! Beech

tors fly most aircraft types, and land and take off from carriers, but cannot serve in a Carrier Air Wing because US law forbids their participating in combat.

While we are talking about restrictions, here's a word of caution to non-American readers: to win wings of gold as a US Navy pilot or NFO, Beth and Joe *must* be American citizens. Recruiters are inundated with mail from buffs in other countries who would like to fly US Navy aircraft.

To get wings of gold in their separate pipelines, aspiring aviators and NFOs: become naval officers; go through aviation indoctrination (AI); and receive primary flight training (for pilots) or basic and intermediate flight training (for NFOs). After that, there are some additional steps as our SNAs (student naval aviators) and SNFOs get to the advanced stages.

Becoming naval officers

The US Navy has no fewer than eleven ways a person can become a commissioned officer.

The traditional method is four years of college-level education and officer training at the US Naval Academy located along the scenic Severn River in Annapolis, Maryland—where ivy clings to hallowed halls and a symbolic F-4 Phantom is on outdoor display. Many believe that the US Navy is run by Annapolis graduates and that a new ensign fresh from the academy is somehow a little more "equal" than the ensign who became an officer one of ten other ways.

Our two exemplars, however, became ensigns via different means. Beth Murray went to a private university and enrolled in Naval Reserve Officer Training Corps (NROTC) which provides not ony training but a stipend during the final two years of college. Beth, as we shall see, is thus an ensign in the Navy before she arrives at Pensacola.

Joe Fives, our second future flier, follows the better-known non-Annapolis route. Like Richard Gere in *An Officer and a Gentleman*, Joe begins in AOCS (Aviation Officer Candidate School). Hollywood placed AOCS in the Pacific Northwest but it's really at Pensacola.

The long, winding road from civilian life to naval flier may end up in the cockpit of a carrier-based, supersonic F-14 Tomcat like this fighter of the "Diamondbacks" of fighter squadron VF-102 settled on the steam catapult aboard USS America (CV-66). To get where they are today, pilot Puke and naval flight officer Ratbreath went through their generation's equivalent of the difficult training regimen described in this volume.

For fourteen weeks, Joe is introduced to military life and discipline by a rough-tough Marine Corps drill instructor (DI), MSGT John Crankshaw. Crankshaw uses no profanity, no physical abuse. "Still," Joe will admit later, "there are times when he made me feel as small as a worm." Visitors to Pensacola invariably turn their heads at the sight of AOCS cadets drilling in formation, even in the blazing heat of summer in the

The name of the game, in the end, is to fly. Capt. Ronald (Taco) Johnson and Capt. Michael (Omar) Bradley may be the envy of would-be naval aviators as they prepare an F–14A Tomcat for takeoff at Miramar Naval Air Station in California. As it happens, however, the pair got into a Navy jet via a different route than that described in this book: both are Air Force officers on an exchange tour. USN

The protagonist of our story is the young American seeking to fly for the Navy, seen here in the person of an SNA (student naval aviator) just after a flight in the Beech T–34C Mentor. Patch on his flight suit extols the merits of VT–6 at Whiting Field, Florida, one of four squadrons which gave primary pilot training in the T–34C. Rob Ketchell

Florida panhandle, their Marine DI humping along beside them, counting cadence.

Crankshaw is a demanding taskmaster. Previously endowed with a fair amount of confidence, Joe Fives feels increasing uncertainty as AOCS unfolds. "I started to wonder if I could do anything right—straighten my bunk, shine my shoes, square my shoulders. If I couldn't pass a barracks inspection, how the heck was I going to fly a Tomcat?"

Joe becomes one of the sixty-five percent of candidates who survive AOCS, which will be covered further in our next chapter. Included in his AOCS pro-

For many who want to fly in the Navy, the first test comes with Aviation Officer Candidate School, where students spend fourteen weeks learning about military life and receiving a mental and physical workout. For some, the biggest challenge comes on the obstacle course, where this AOCS student is struggling through the sand. Peter B. Mersky

Before the future naval aviator or naval flight officer can take to the skies, the process of becoming an officer will demand brainpower, toil, and sweat. At Pensacola, these aviation officer candidates stand at parade rest during graduation ceremonies for a more advanced class. They are learning military ways in the barracks and on the parade ground, while soaking up naval terminology and traditions in the classroom. USN/JOCS Kirby Harrison

gram is six weeks of Aviation Indoctrination (AI) which is given separately in a six-week program to Beth and others who are already officers. AI studies include aerodynamics, navigation, flight physiology, and water and land survival training.

Of course our future fliers are permitted to look up when an airplane flies over. In addition to a superb air museum, at Pensacola they'll see Rockwell T-2B Buckeyes, Douglas TA-4J Skyhawks and Cessna T-47A Citations. Neighboring Whiting Field has Beech T-34C Turbo Mentors, used for primary pilot training (all "primary" is done at Whiting or NAS Corpus Christi, Texas, and the T-34C has an excellent reputation as a flier's first airplane).

Beth Murray offends no one by dreaming the impossible dream: of the various flight training programs, Beth wants to go through the strike syllabus— the program covering fighter and attack pilots. Even in the 1990s, with the segregated WAVE Corps a relic of the past and women an integral part of the US armed forces, Beth's goal will be difficult to attain.

Primary and Basic

It's often hinted, darkly, that NFOs are second-class citizens, a notch above mere groundlings but not gifted enough to qualify as pilots. That's rubbish. But it's true that some NFOs have wanted to be pilots and couldn't see well enough. A pilot ordinarily must have 20/20 vision, uncorrected. The requirement for an NFO is less strict. It's debatable whether this makes sense but it's a fact of life. Joe Fives was one of those who wanted to be a pilot but whose vision forces him

next page
The intensity and seriousness of AOCS is reflected on the faces of these Aviation Officer Candidates, marching with a folded flag in preparation for a flag-raising ceremony at Pensacola. Attention to every aspect of uniform appearance and dress, from polished hat brim to polished shoes, is an inescapable reality throughout every moment of AOCS. USN

The "big picture" for future naval aviators never loses sight of the fact that most of the earth's surface is water and the Navy operates over water. Water survival training is part of Navy life for everybody, and a recurring event for *future naval aviators. At NAS Miramar, California, a female Reserve Officer Training Corps (ROTC) midshipman and future aviator, in full flight gear, attempts to climb into a life raft during water survival training. USN*

to seek an NFO rating. But Joe need not pack his suitcase just yet.

At stage two, all prospective NFOs are still together. Stage two is a move across the field to the "Cosmic Cats" of Squadron VT-10 at Pensacola. VT-10 uses T-34C Turbo Mentors to provide fourteen weeks of basic NFO training, including twelve flight hours and twenty-five hours in simulators. Naturally, Joe breezes through.

Transferred to NAS Whiting Field in nearby Milton, Florida, pilot trainee Beth Murray breezes through her stage two—primary pilot training.

All future Navy pilots begin actual flying in "primary," conducted mostly at Whiting Field and at Corpus Christi (chapter 3). In primary, students finally learn whether they're comfortable at the controls of a metal machine hurtling through emptiness in the high open spaces above Florida's perpetual sun. Beth has done some civilian flying and, while opinions differ as to its utility, she is at ease when an instructor starts her through dual-control training in the Beech T-34C.

Beth makes her first solo in the Beech T-34C after ten hours of flight time and thirteen flights. For many, this is the big test. Student pilots will have memorable experiences thereafter, but the first solo is special.

next page
In primary flight training, future naval aviators struggle through academic and simulator work and learn to fly the Beech T-34C Turbo Mentor. The student aviator in this photo performs the pre-flight checks on a T-34C. Peter B. Mersky

For Beth, it is a magic moment. The air is smooth as glass. The T-34C hums like a sewing machine.

Most naval flying, especially during training, goes smoothly. Once in awhile, though, something happens to remind student and instructor alike that flying requires a readiness for emergency.

During a T-34C flight near Whiting Field, Captain Carl J. Jenkins of the "Doer Birds" of VT-2 (one of many Marines who are naval aviators) told his student, Ensign Jeffrey W. Blackmer, to execute an approach turn stall maneuver. Blackmer went into the maneuver at 7,500 feet and when maximum power was applied for recovery, the engine suffered a catastrophic failure. All power was lost and forward visibility was obscured by oil. Jenkins took control and immediately executed high-altitude power-loss procedures.

With no airfield within gliding distance and over a heavily forested area, Captain Jenkins selected the only available landing site, a 1,500-foot pasture. He maneuvered the T-34C to a high-key position over the field and made a flawless gear-up, flaps-down dead stick landing into the field which was ringed by tall pine trees. Jenkins slipped the T-34C over the tall pines to a touchdown 500 feet down the field, slid 800 feet and came to rest 200 feet short of the trees at the end of the field.

Their adventure was unfinished; when the two crewmen exited the T-34C, they were confronted by an irate bull upset over having his herd disturbed. Another T-34C flew cover and neutralized the threat, enabling the two aviators to beat a hasty retreat. It was learned later that a seemingly minor turbine blade problem was the cause of their unexpected belly landing.

Intermediate

Now comes the stage three—the first time Joe Fives and fellow NFO candidates must separate. A few will become navigators (SNFOs) on the long antisubmarine patrols flown in the Lockheed P-3C Orion. These SNFOs pack their bags and cross the country for twenty-two weeks of navigator training in the Boeing T-43 (a military 737) with the Air Force at Mather

After the T-34C, next step for the future pilot is the North American T-2C Buckeye jet trainer used for the intermediate strike syllabus. This SNA is shown climbing aboard a Buckeye for a training hop at NAS Meridian, Mississippi, one of three locations where this phase of training is offered. Rob Ketchell

AFB, California. This program includes eighty flight hours and seventy-two simulator hours. To his everlasting joy, Joe is not chosen.

After basic, VT-10's "Cosmic Cats" provide intermediate NFO training with T-34Cs, T-2Bs and T-47As. The Buckeyes are the only B models in inventory. Joe and his fellow candidates are split into four groups, who now know what type of aircraft they will fly if they succeed with their further training: overwater jet navigator (OJN) candidates will crew the Lockheed S-3 Viking; advanced tactical data systems (ATDS) candidates will serve aboard the Grumman E-2C Hawkeye; tactical navigators (TN) will occupy the right seat in the Grumman A-6E Intruder. To make our story even more complex, a proportion of these candidates will go on to airborne electronic warfare (ALEW) school to serve aboard the Grumman EA-6B Prowler. Finally, in the group Joe Fives has successfully joined, radar intercept officer (RIO) candidates will be back-seaters in the incomparable Grumman F-14 Tomcat.

Joe is quiet and studious, and his biggest worry, as he practices flying tactics with VT-10's assortment of intermediate trainers, is what happens if he fails. At this juncture, few prospective NFOs do fail, and Joe's worries are within healthy bounds.

Just as NFO candidates had to separate, so too must future pilots. After whetting their teeth on the T-34C, student aviators separate into three pipelines—strike, maritime and rotary wing. Strike leads to assignment to carrier-based jet aircraft (A-6, A-7, F-14, F-18 and S-3). The maritime pipeline readies the candidate for multi-engine turboprop aircraft (P-3, C-130 and others). Rotary wing training leads to helicopters (SH-2, SH-3, CH-46, RH-53 and MH-53). To again introduce a further element of confusion, a few candidates scheduled for the turboprop Grumman E-2 Hawkeye early-warning aircraft and C-2A Greyhound carrier on-board delivery (COD) aircraft will follow a unique path through parts of both the maritime and strike pipelines.

Beth Murray is in seventh heaven. For Beth, stage three is a move to McCain Field, NAS Meridian, Mississippi, for the challenge of basic jet training in preparation for assignment to the strike community. She has become a unique person in naval aviation—training for a mission women are not yet allowed to perform. Up front, she knows that even if she does very well undergoing approximately 100 hours in the T-2C, even if she advances to the TA-4J Skyhawk, she cannot live aboard a carrier or be a member of a Carrier Air Wing.

Strike candidates transfer to one of four training wings at Pensacola, Meridian, or Kingsville or Beeville, Texas. Newly assigned to the "Green Frogs" of VT-19, Beth turns out to have a natural touch on the Rockwell T-2C Buckeye.

Beth and others aspiring to fly fighter and attack aircraft must undergo rigorous study of meteorology, communications, aerodynamics, engineering and navigation, as well as stress-prone work in the 2F-101 flight simulator. But the high point of strike is flying at speeds in excess of 400 mph at 30,000 feet and getting the hang of formation flying, aerobatics, jet maneuvering, and visual and instrument navigation. The T-2C Buckeye has a roomy cockpit, analog instruments and a "heavy feel"; in some ways it is more of a challenge than the fighters or attack planes our SNA will fly in the future. Toward the end of the strike syllabus, our student undergoes gunnery and carrier qualification aboard the flattop USS Lexington (CVT-16).

That first carrier landing—becoming a bona fide "tailhooker"—is another crucial milestone. Beth and her cohorts receive exhaustive briefings on the optical landing system from an LSO (landing signal officer). After two field-practice carrier landings (FCLPs) with an instructor, they are unleashed to land solo on the airfield's simulated carrier deck. Then, Beth pilots the T-2C out to Lady Lex. Following the syllabus, she completes two touch-and-go landings, four arrested landings and four catapult launches.

It was during an intended catapult launch from the Lexington that LTJG James B. Clark II of the "Professionals" of VT-23 had a decidedly uncharacteristic experience. During his initial T-2C carrier qualifications, Clark was spotted on the No. 1 catapult for launch. Following a normal run-up he saluted the catapult officer, indicating his readiness for launch. When the catapult fired, the port-side bridle loop separated from the aircraft bridle hook, slewing the T-2C thirty degrees leftward and making the starboard bridle loop disengage from the aircraft.

Jim Clark reduced power instantly and applied maximum brakes, bringing the Buckeye to a halt two-thirds down the catapult track, less than ten feet from

next page
There may be some experience better than landing on a carrier—but probably not. TA-4J Skyhawk trainer from VT-7 settles down on the boat. Douglas/Harry Gann

a turning Grumman C–2A Greyhound carrier on-board delivery (COD) transport with eighteen people on board.

Clark's instantaneous and correct response to this extremely time-critical emergency clearly saved

The Navy is within a percentage point or two of having more helicopters than fixed-wing airplanes, and the training of helicopter pilots is vital. A chopper pilot watches his CH–46 Sea Knight being fueled, the kind of scene which will become routine in the Fleet for students who finish the rotary wing syllabus at NAS Whiting Field. USN

his T–2C Buckeye and possibly the COD and its passengers as well.

Meanwhile, back at Pensacola, SNFO Joe Fives has slipped the surly bonds. He is also strapped inside a T–2 Buckeye, one of the B models still in service. His apprehension swept away, he finds that he can handle the sensation of flight—some never adjust to flying, which is inherently not a natural act—and he doesn't become ill or disoriented when the T–2B pilot "yanks and banks" at high speed. Some NFO candidates call the T–2B a "vomit comet," but Joe finds that he's comfortable and at ease sitting out in the back while fighter maneuvers are imitated.

Intermediate for Joe means twelve hours in the T–2B, ten in the T–34C and twelve in the Cessna T–47A Platypus. Our SNFO now is exposed to instrument navigation on airways, instrument approaches, low-level/high-speed visual navigation and crew co-ordination.

Advanced

Ensign Joe Fives is now ready for advanced training in the RIO (radar intercept officer) pipeline. Still at Pensacola, he joins the "Sabre Hawks" of VT–86, equipped with TA–4J Skyhawks and T–47As. Here, Joe undergoes aircraft, simulator and classroom training to learn the fine art of aerial intercepts. This syllabus includes forty-six hours in the T–47A and six hours of advanced tactical maneuvering in the TA–4J.

In the advanced stage, Joe begins to notice something odd. People are beginning to treat him like an adult. At the dark beginning at AOCS, where Sergeant Crankshaw was likely to compare him with the lowliest form of insect life, Joe had one heck of a time maintaining self-esteem. In the cockpit of a TA–4J blasting through the ever-pristine Florida skies at Mach 0.8 and faster, Joe is being treated like a naval officer. People are saluting him, as they were supposed to all along. Once in awhile, an instructor actually bestows a compliment.

Beth Murray remains at Meridian, joins the "Eagles" of VT–7 and checks out in the TA–4J Skyhawk. The advanced strike syllabus is no country picnic. Over 24.6 weeks (only the US Navy can divide a week into tenths!), Beth receives 108 hours in the TA–4J, sixty-eight in simulators and a stupendous amount of "booklearning." It hasn't gotten any easier, but Beth, too, notices that instructors and station cadre are beginning to treat her like a real person rather than some wet-behind-the-ears kid. Salutes from enlisted sailors are snappier, compliments from senior officers more frequent. Murray, too, begins to feel like a real naval aviator.

In the weapons stage, Murray learns to aim, accurately, bombs, rockets and bullets at a ground target. Because modern warfare is low and fast, she learns to fly the TA-4J at low altitudes and high speeds. She practices air combat maneuvering (ACM), and afterward, the syllabus includes six arrested landings and catapult shots from *Lady Lex* in the TA-4J.

Had she not chosen the strike syllabus, she might have gone to advanced E-2/C-2 multi-engine training which in 5.6 weeks provides seventeen hours in the Beech T-44A Pegasus and eleven in simulators. Or she might have gone to advanced maritime training (for future P-3 pilots)—18.6 weeks, eighty-eight hours in the T-44A, thirty in simulators. Or she might have gone to advanced helicopter training—22.2 weeks, 116 hours in the Bell TH-57A Sea Ranger, twenty-four in simulators. All of these pathways end with the naval aviator acquiring wings and preparing to serve operationally.

Wings of gold

For pilots, the wings of gold come after eighteen months, 270 flight hours and many more of exhaust-ing classroom work. Once training is finished, the new naval aviator proceeds to the FRS (fleet replenishment squadron, still commonly called a "Rag" after the older term "replacement air group") for the type of aircraft he or she will fly. Some aircraft types have a "Rag" on each coast, one each for the Atlantic and Pacific fleets.

If our twisted tale of naval aviator training had a perfect ending, Murray and Fives might find themselves together again in an FRS squadron. In fact, Fives was introduced to the F-14A Tomcat in such a squadron, the "Grim Reapers" of VF-101 at NAS Oceana, Virginia, and now flies with the "Diamondbacks" of VF-102. In real life, a minor medical situation delays Murray and she is still at Meridian as this appears—in final training to pilot a Tomcat, Hornet or Intruder.

In the 1990s, the intermediate and advanced pilot and NFO training now provided by the T-2B and T-2C Buckeye and the TA-4J Skyhawk will be taken over by a single aircraft, the Douglas T-45A Goshawk, the aircraft part of a T-45TS (training system). It was once thought that the T-45A, a license-built variant of

The maritime pipeline takes student naval aviators from the Beech T-34 Turbo Mentor through the twin-engine Beech T-44 Pegasus, and prepares them to fly the Lockheed P-3C Orion anti-submarine warfare aircraft. This P-3C is in a shallow bank during a flight along a coastline. USN

the British Aerospace Hawk, would begin to reach Naval Air Training Command by as early as 1986. Difficulties are being addressed and the "Fighting Redhawks" of VT-21 at Kingsville are scheduled to receive their twelfth T-45A, giving them IOC (initial operating capability) in June 1991.

Delays with the T-45A are partly attributable to the problems of making a land-based aircraft operable from carrier decks. "You can take a carrier plane and modify it for use on land," says one naval officer. "Doing it the other way is harder."

The US Navy chose the Hawk as its new pilot trainer in November 1981 and agreed to buy fifty-four airframes made in Britain to hasten delivery and enable the Hawk to go into service in 1986. The remaining airframes in an order for 302 (plus flight simulators and other components in the system) would be manufactured in Long Beach, California, by Douglas.

The plan to include British-manufactured airplanes did not survive deliberations in the US Congress, this being the cause of at least some delay in the program.

On 20 November 1983, *The Sunday Times* noted that because the US Navy wanted an "all wet" Hawk—that is, one fully capable of carrier operations, the aircraft would not be in service until 1988. In fact, the first Douglas T-45A Goshawk was rolled out at Long Beach on 16 March 1988 and flew there on 19 April 1988. In mid-1989 two airframes were undergoing tests at NAS Patuxent River, Maryland. IOC, scheduled for September 1990, was pushed back to June 1991. As this volume went to press, it was understood the date had slipped again to June 1992.

The T-45A Goshawk—the American version of which differs from the British version in having a twin nosewheel and tailhook—is a superb aircraft and will be valuable well into the next century. However, the original buy was made in the heady Reagan years when the Defense Department seemed to have unlimited funds. In the current budget climate, any trainer aircraft is vulnerable to the budget ax, and a strong possibility exists that the number of T-45As obtained could be less than was once foreseen.

Briefly, that is an overview of US naval aviator training today. It does not do justice to the intensity of the training schemes—the four to six hours of preparation for every hour of flight time, the mind-bending pressure on students to perform at every juncture, the confidence-building measures thrown into the program for the pilot who might, some night, approach a carrier in zero-zero weather with one set of controls and one pair of eyes. It is an experience most enjoy—at least when looking back at it. Joe Fives is now a back-seater in an F-14 Tomcat of the VF-102 "Diamondbacks" aboard USS *America* (CV-66), and he says, "I wouldn't trade anything for it."

US Navy Flight Training

Wing	Base	Squadron	Tailcode	Side Numbers	Aircraft	Nickname	Notes
TW-1	NAS Meridian, Mississippi (McCain Field)	VT-7	A	7XX	TA-4J, A-4E	"Eagles"	Advanced Jet (pilot)
		VT-19	A	5XX	T-2C	"Green Frogs"	Basic Jet (pilot)
TW-2	NAS Kingsville, Texas	VT-21	B	1XX	TA-4J	"Fighting Redhawks"	Advanced Jet (pilot)
		VT-22	B	1XX	TA-4J	"Golden Eagles"	Advanced Jet (pilot)
		VT-23	B	3XX	T-2C	"Professionals"	Basic Jet (pilot)
TW-3	NAS Beeville, Texas (Chase Field)	VT-24	C	4XX	TA-4J	"Bobcats"	Advanced Jet (pilot)
		VT-25	C	5XX	TA-4J	"Cougars"	Advanced Jet (pilot)
		VT-26	C	6XX	T-2C	"Tigers"	Basic Jet (pilot)
TW-4	NAS Corpus Christi, Texas (Cabaniss Field)	VT-27	G(*)	7XX	T-34C	"Boomers"	Primary Flight (pilot)
		VT-28	G	8XX	T-44A	"Rangers"	Multi-engine Flight (pilot)
		VT-31	G	1XX	T-44A	"Wise Owls"	Multi-engine Flight (pilot)
TW-5	NAS Whiting Field, Milton, Florida	VT-2	E	5XX	T-34C	"Doer Birds"	Primary Flight (pilot)
		VT-3	E	2XX	T-34C	"Red Knights"	Primary Flight (pilot)
		VT-6	E	2XX	T-34C	(None)	Intermediate Prop (helicopter)
		HT-8	E	0XX	TH-57A	(None)	Transition Helicopter
		HT-18	E	1XX	TH-57A	(None)	Advanced Helicopter

US Navy Flight Training

Wing	Base	Squadron	Tailcode	Side Numbers	Aircraft	Nickname	Notes
TW-6	NAS Pensacola, Florida	VT-4	F	3XX (T-2) 36X (TA-4J)	T-2C, TA-4J	(None)	Basic Jet; Advanced Jet
		VT-10	F	01-15 (T-47)	T-2B, T-47A	"Cosmic Cats"	Basic (T-2) and Intermediate NFO
		VT-86	F	23X (TA-4J)	TA-4J, T-47A	"Sabre Hawks"	RIO, Tactical Navigator Overwater Jet Navigator (NFO)

(*) *Tailcode was originally D (Delta) but in radio communications was confused with Delta Air Lines.*

Naval Undergraduate Pilot Training Programs

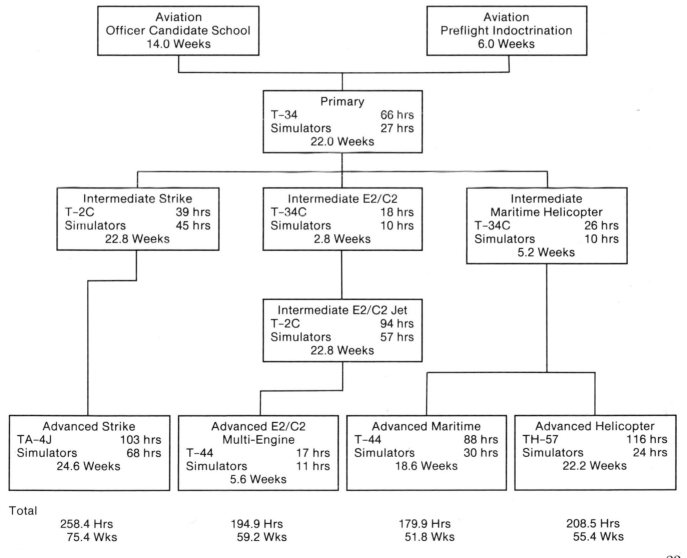

	Aviation Officer Candidate School 14.0 Weeks		Aviation Preflight Indoctrination 6.0 Weeks	

Primary
T-34   66 hrs
Simulators   27 hrs
22.0 Weeks

Intermediate Strike
T-2C   39 hrs
Simulators   45 hrs
22.8 Weeks

Intermediate E2/C2
T-34C   18 hrs
Simulators   10 hrs
2.8 Weeks

Intermediate Maritime Helicopter
T-34C   26 hrs
Simulators   10 hrs
5.2 Weeks

Intermediate E2/C2 Jet
T-2C   94 hrs
Simulators   57 hrs
22.8 Weeks

Advanced Strike
TA-4J   103 hrs
Simulators   68 hrs
24.6 Weeks

Advanced E2/C2 Multi-Engine
T-44   17 hrs
Simulators   11 hrs
5.6 Weeks

Advanced Maritime
T-44   88 hrs
Simulators   30 hrs
18.6 Weeks

Advanced Helicopter
TH-57   116 hrs
Simulators   24 hrs
22.2 Weeks

Total

| 258.4 Hrs | 194.9 Hrs | 179.9 Hrs | 208.5 Hrs |
| 75.4 Wks | 59.2 Wks | 51.8 Wks | 55.4 Wks |

Undergraduate Naval Flight Officer Programs

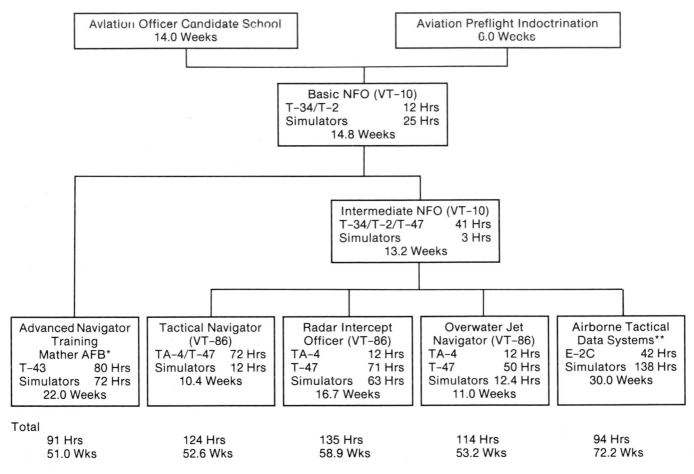

| Aviation Officer Candidate School 14.0 Weeks | | Aviation Preflight Indoctrination 6.0 Weeks |

Basic NFO (VT-10)
T-34/T-2   12 Hrs
Simulators   25 Hrs
14.8 Weeks

Intermediate NFO (VT-10)
T-34/T-2/T-47   41 Hrs
Simulators   3 Hrs
13.2 Weeks

Advanced Navigator Training Mather AFB*	Tactical Navigator (VT-86)	Radar Intercept Officer (VT-86)	Overwater Jet Navigator (VT-86)	Airborne Tactical Data Systems**
T-43 80 Hrs Simulators 72 Hrs 22.0 Weeks	TA-4/T-47 72 Hrs Simulators 12 Hrs 10.4 Weeks	TA-4 12 Hrs T-47 71 Hrs Simulators 63 Hrs 16.7 Weeks	TA-4 12 Hrs T-47 50 Hrs Simulators 12.4 Hrs 11.0 Weeks	E-2C 42 Hrs Simulators 138 Hrs 30.0 Weeks
Total 91 Hrs 51.0 Wks	124 Hrs 52.6 Wks	135 Hrs 58.9 Wks	114 Hrs 53.2 Wks	94 Hrs 72.2 Wks

*Joint Navy/USAF training at Sacramento, California.
**Undergraduate training done at RVAW-110 Miramar and RVAW-120 Norfolk.

Chapter 2

Aviation Officer Cadet School and Aviation Preflight Indoctrination

The city of Pensacola in the Florida panhandle is the cradle of naval aviation. When the US joined the First World War in 1917, Pensacola was the only naval air station and the home of all of the Navy's forty-eight aviators and fifty-four aircraft. Since before the Second World War, Pensacola has been where the best and brightest train, learn and fly.

Many future Navy fliers come to make the transformation from civilian to naval officer. These men and women are students at AOCS (Aviation Officer

From the very first, even before being issued naval attire, the new AOCS candidate learns to march in formation, call cadence, and maintain a military bearing. For their first week, these candidates will be "Poopies" and will get a dramatic introduction to life in the Navy. Rob Ketchell

Candidate School)—that fourteen-week pressure cooker which takes 1,400 men and women each year and molds those who have the right stuff into naval officers. AOCS also weeds out those who can't cut it.

Two paths lead to Pensacola and to AOCS. The first and largest group of AOCS students consists of aviation officer candidates who have a college degree and will be commissioned as ensigns after the fourteen-week school and before beginning flight training. This group includes not only future pilots and naval flight officers (NFOs) who are the focus of our story but also men and women who will serve as aviation intelligence officers and aviation maintenance duty officers.

The second group is made up of Naval Aviation Cadets (Navcads) who have at least two years of college. These too are future pilots and NFOs, but Navcads will be commissioned only after completing flight training—on the same day they receive their wings. These young Americans have a military obligation to complete in the enlisted ranks if they fail in aviator training, so they are fiercely motivated.

This man is the personification of all the misery, struggle, and ultimate triumph of the future Navy pilot or Naval Flight Officer during those grueling weeks of AOCS. The Marine DI, or drill instructor, is supposed to look and act mean. In fact, the DI needs to be not only a taskmaster but, in addition, a combination of chaplain, psychologist and diplomat, fully equipped for every kind of "people" problem. USN

When you learn you're going to AOCS, the Navy sends you a nice booklet which begins with "Congratulations!" It's appropriate. To get through the difficult selection process, you've needed health, intelligence and motivation. The standards are exceedingly high. Those who qualify for a slot at AOCS are special. "We're seeing the real cream of American youth," says a senior Navy officer. "These young people are so capable, it's amazing." The rigorous military and athletic training and the academic courses at AOCS are intense; cautions the Navy, "Self-discipline will be required."

Although the Florida panhandle seldom gets snow, temperatures can still get down to freezing. If you go through AOCS in February it will be damp, dark and cold when the rock-tough Marine DI (drill instructor) rousts everybody out of their bunks. Summers are sizzling in Pensacola and the temperature can zoom to 95 degrees in the shade. If you go through AOCS in July, you will remember the sweat, the ever-present sweat, the endless push-ups, the PT (physical training), wearing you down, exhausting you.

That's how it was for Richard Gere in Hollywood's *An Officer and a Gentleman*. But in real life it is both different and harder. Says AOCS graduate Laine Konrad, "At the end of Poopie Week—that's your first week in AOCS—you've been PT'ed so much you can't reach to your back pocket without your arms hurting." Konrad's advice: "Walk in strong already. You'll need to be strong. Don't expect them to build you up."

You also need to be prepared for what seems, at first, public humiliation. Much of this comes from your stern-faced, iron-eyed Marine Corps drill instructor. The DI looms in front of the group and announces, "The following people cannot cut it"—and begins rattling off names of those being given demerits for infractions.

Barracks for AOCS's Battalions I and II are large southern plantation mansions that are, for the most part, red brick with long white pillars stretching from the ground to the roof of the two-story building. To one observer, the barracks conveyed a sense of fraternity. "They even looked like a high-class frat house at Yale or Harvard."

The first day in AOCS, you realize that they're going to get you physically and mentally beat. It starts with the crashing of the garbage cans. The DI paces back and forth, clanging the barracks' garbage cans and shouting, "Get up, get up!" Dazed, sleepy-eyed aviation officer candidates rush from their rooms in time to see a garbage can and lid come bouncing down the hall, banging all the way. One of the candidates is a little slow and the DI snaps at him, "Five and down on the floor!" The hapless candidate begins the first push-ups of many to be ordered in the days ahead. There are always push-ups. It's PT and as one candidate puts it, "They PT you in the morning, afternoon, before dinner, after dinner . . ."

That first morning, the candidates do not yet have uniforms. Clad in a mix of jeans and sport clothes, they are slow responding. "No! Not fast enough!" the DI shouts. "Try it again!"

New candidates are surprisingly quick to learn and adapt. One of the authors saw new candidates still in civilian clothes, their hair not yet shaved by the barber, already shouting out, "Yes, sir!" and bracing at attention as if they'd been doing it for weeks.

Difficult as it is to get to AOCS, some candidates actually DOR (drop on request), or quit, the first day. Twenty-four percent of those arriving at AOCS will drop in the first week, most as a result of not being physically qualified, or for personal reasons. Another eleven percent will be lost by attrition in the remainder of the AOCS program. The sixty-five percent who survive AOCS obviously are highly motivated.

This AOCS candidate is confronted with double trouble— not one but two drill instructors reviewing his military bearing. Though they give the impression of being emotional, DIs are thoroughly professional and always under control. USN

At all times, at all hours, AOCS students feel the presence of the DI. A newly-arrived officer candidate is about to hit the deck for push-ups under the direction of his Marine Corps drill instructor. USN

On The Mark
By ENS Mark Hutchins

Ensign Mark Hutchins earned his Navy commission earlier this year through the NROTC program at Rennesalear Polytechnic Institute while studying at nearby Union College in Schenectady, New York. The Brunswick, Maine native is in Aviation Indoctrination Training at NAS Pensacola at this writing. Before he began his quest for wings he was "stashed" at the Navy Military Personnel Command awaiting a slot at Pensacola. Wings of Gold asked Mark to express some "pre-training command" thoughts. This is the first in a series of articles by flight students on the pathway to the gold wings of naval aviators and naval flight officers.

I was at NAS Oceana, Virginia during my second class NROTC cruise when I got a right seat hop in a VA–85 A–6 Intruder for a practice bombing mission on a target in North Carolina. It was absolutely great! I had flown in a T–2 Buckeye on a field trip to Corpus Christi the previous spring and was impressed with that jet. The A–6, of course, was something else. I liked the big cockpit, the excellent visibility and all that power.

On the bombing runs the pilot executed pop-up and loft maneuvers. Later we did some aerobatics. I was so enthralled with the experience that after we landed I was ready to go right back up again. I'm not one of those people who claim they wanted to fly ever since they were a kid. But since that day in the *Intruder* I knew, without any doubt, that I wanted to be an aviator in the Navy. I want to learn a lot and have fun. I believe that aviation will satisfy those twin desires.

As for duty in Washington before entering the training command pipeline, I asked for it. A friend told me that having a nice apartment, good times and getting per diem checks would make the assignment memorable. Belatedly, I learned that per diem wasn't a part of the deal. And the cost of nice apartments in the area was out of sight. But I did get a glimpse of the bureaucracy and how the Navy handles its people at the headquarters level.

I was assigned to the Air Combat Placement office in the Navy Annex, not the Pentagon. The annex isn't exactly an architectural masterpiece but a lot happens inside those walls that affect the officers and enlisted personnel in the fleet. I assisted the Flight Student Placement Officer (NMPC–433E). I dealt with flight students every day, got a good feel for their problems and aspirations. The phone rang a lot and there were times I felt more like a secretary than an NFO-to-be. But what I learned helped me understand the overall picture of what Naval Air is all about.

A couple of students already in the pipeline insisted that prior flight experience and hitting the books before checking in were good ways to get a leg up on the syllabus. Others told me that neither of those actions were necessary. Hard work was the main key to success, along with not getting distracted by various temptations along the way. Everyone agrees that the competition in the training command is intense. No surprise there.

To me its all a matter of setting the right standards for myself and striving to live up to them. I may have to adjust but for now my goal is to give it everything I've got, all the while keeping my eyes on the big prize: those precious wings of gold.

First printed in Wings of Gold, *Winter 1988*

Poopie Week

Poopie Week, those first seven days at AOCS when the going is toughest, candidates wear ill-fitting green pants, a T-shirt which must be kept snow-white and the requisite Poopie Chrome Dome (a silver helmet liner) over their shaved heads. The physical demands are constant, the punitive PT incessant. Konrad says, "I remember one guy doing PT when we were on the bus en route to pick up our flight boots."

In fact, candidates almost never ride a bus. They march everywhere. Their military formation has the right-of-way when crossing a road. As part of introduction to military ways—or, as some see it, torture—road guards from the formation run ahead and stand in the middle of traffic lanes to stop all vehicles. Once the slow-moving formation has marched across the road, the DI barks out an order and the guards hustle to rejoin. It is movement, movement, movement. You're never still. You never rest.

There is no talking during meals. There is no rest, ever. After lights out at 9 p.m., candidates grope around trying to make preparations for the next time they get RLP'ed (subjected to a room, locker and personnel inspection). There is seldom time for much sleep.

In official jargon, Poopie Week is called INDOC—short for indoctrination. Says the Navy: "You are met on the first morning of INDOC by a Marine Corps drill instructor. From that minute, every part of every day is regimented. You'll get uniforms, haircuts, and intense military and physical training that includes swimming.

"There is no free time during INDOC. No mail or phone calls, except in time of emergency, are permitted until Sunday of INDOC week.

"Physical, mental and emotional limits are tested. Only those with that extra determination endure and succeed."

Poopie Week is the first and last seven days of the prospective naval aviator's life when no academic work is expected. You eat, you march, you do PT, you wear the heavy and annoying helmet. You learn to polish brass.

Is this some form of madness? Are the Marine DIs sadists, bent upon destroying the bodies and minds of young people?

In fact, of course, the DIs don't hate anyone and aren't sadistic. They are professionals, hand-picked from the top one to five percent of Marine enlisted ranks and rigorously trained to test candidates to the limit. They can turn on and turn off their menacing tone in an instant.

A drill instructor checks an AOCS candidate's haircut and posture. USN

Poopies on the march in front of Aviation Schools Command's red brick building at Pensacola. For the first week, *civilian garb is replaced by green pants, white T-shirts and Poopie Chrome Dome.* Rob Ketchell

Candidates quickly learn that the DI is in charge. "You'll see a lot of me in the next fourteen weeks," the DI warns that first day. "I'm going to teach you how to march, how to wear your uniforms properly and how to make your bunks. I won't teach you to fly. Hopefully, you'll learn that later if you're still around. Right now I'll teach you enough discipline to keep you from embarrassing yourselves when you get to your squadrons."

During Poopie Week, the candidate quickly learns that he or she cannot cope with this pressure alone. This is the DI's objective—to stress you out so much that you'll turn to the other candidates for reinforcement. You'll function as a team.

Consider, for example, the way the DI goes through the barracks doling out demerits and looking for unsecured lockers. The student's M-1 rifle is kept in the locker and woe to any candidate who leaves his door open.

AOCS graduate Peter Mersky: "I remember a young man dashing the entire length of the building to the head, holding his M-1 at port arms, upright, its barrel completely inundated with Brasso metal polish. The DIs had found his locker unlocked and treated his weapon to a Brasso bath. Only a quick shower could keep the polish from hopelessly drying and that's where this quick-thinking individual was headed, clothes and all."

Mersky makes his point: "Details. Details. That's what it's all about. Remembering a small thing, like securing your locker, might teach you to remember details in the air which might save your life or your

The rigors of military life are never forgotten in AOCS, not even at dinner time. Officer candidates brace at attention at the conclusion of a meal. USN

plane, or both. In fact that's where all of the AOCS program [leads], attention to detail."

At the end of Poopie Week, all of the DIs join your own DI for a shattering climax to your initiation—a rigorous inspection and an almost certain tongue-lashing for any infraction.

After this final Poopie RLP, you throw everything into a bag and get moved to a new building where the rest of the classes are located in what's known as the "death march." This is the ultimate in physical stress—being paraded in the July heat (or February chill) with all of your gear, struggling, sweating, always sweating. "Twenty percent of us are puking," says Konrad. Possibly Konrad exaggerates. Yet this is a controlled situation. "It is *not* unsafe . . ."

A student who'd survived all this and begun flight training looked back at the "death march" and shared his recollection with one of the authors. "The DI made us pack our gear into a duffel bag and march for two hours around a square block.

"The DI was always in complete—ominous—control. He would slowly, casually stride around the formation, barking out commands that had the candidates scurrying around as if their very lives depended on complete and proper execution of the order given them.

"As we marched around the block, wherever there was a patch of grass, the DI would disperse us onto the grass for calisthenics. After he thought we were pretty worn out, he would form us up again and march us off to the next patch of grass to do PT over again."

Post-Poopie AOCS

Says the Navy's welcome booklet, "Following INDOC, your class will be assigned to one of two (formerly three) battalions." AOCS candidates live in dormitories, four men or four women to a room. (As the only female in her class, Laine Konrad bunked alone.) Each class is assigned a Marine drill instructor and a class officer, the latter a Navy aviation officer.

That 1983 film *An Officer and a Gentleman* overlooked the emphasis on classroom academics and standards of conduct expected from candidates. The physical part is grueling, but the mind-bending academic work is, if anything, a tougher challenge. Adds one AOCS graduate about the movie: "Also, [in real life] there [is] no time for shacking up and under no circumstances taking on a DI. Besides being flattened [in a Hollywood-style fight with a DI], disciplinary ramifications would be fast and devastating."

At this point, it needs to be mentioned that later in our story we'll be meeting SNAs (student naval

aviators) and SNFOs (student naval flight officers) who didn't go through AOCS. These are young naval officers who were commissioned via some other route—the Naval Academy at Annapolis, Marine Corps PLC (platoon leader course) or college NROTC (naval reserve officer training corps). These future fliers also begin their careers at Pensacola, being introduced to the booklearning side of flying by taking the six-week course called AI (Aviation Indoctrina-

Carrying M1 Garand rifles of the kind lugged by thousands of American GIs during World War II, AOCS students learn the finer points of drill under arms. Khaki garb and M-1s are de rigeur *from the end of Poopie Week to the completion of AOCS thirteen weeks later. The M-1 rifle is no longer in use with US forces but remains an essential feature on the parade ground. Rob Ketchell*

tion). For AOCS candidates, AI is included in the fourteen weeks of their program.

In Aviation Schools Command's large brick class building, the exhausted candidate struggles to prevent falling asleep—a heinous infraction—and receives instructions on the variety of subjects taught at Aviation Schools Command, ranging from the technical (aerodynamics, navigation and power plants) to the informational (naval history, naval orientation and naval justice).

Some subjects are taught at considerable length. Aerodynamics provides a foundation in basic theory upon which actual flight procedures are based. The course in aircraft power plants includes principles and concepts essential to the operation and maintenance of everything from reciprocating engines to jet engines. The basic navigation course provides the prerequisites for the advanced navigation studies to come during the in-flight portion of the training.

Always included on the day's schedule is PT, drill instruction or an RLP inspection. For PT, candidates hurry back to the barracks, change into sweatgear and march off to the gym. Besides calisthenics, candidates become all too familiar with two main athletic courses—the obstacle and cross country courses—which are run two to three times a week each.

Says Mersky: "The Obstacle Course (O-Course) is a tortuous affair made up of eight- and twelve-foot

M1s at "right shoulder arms," these AOCS students march to graduation ceremonies for another class. By this point in their training their attention to detail is so well honed that it is unlikely that any lint or dust dirties their perfectly-pressed uniforms or that the smallest smudge mars the shine on their shoes. USN

bulkheads, rope climbs, log bridges and tire traps (just as in the Gere movie), all to be run in under four minutes, ten seconds. The second course is the Cross Country Course or C-Course. Two miles of undulating territory with sand traps. Qualifying time is about twelve minutes. Endurance is what it's all about, setting a pace, maintaining it and finishing the course."

Captain Steven Ramsdell went back and looked at the O-Course years after running it. "I have no trouble imagining the barrier of pain and exhaustion serious runners must overcome to complete a marathon, and standing before me, quietly asserting its authority, is the barrier every flight student must overcome to enter the fraternity of naval aviation. Both barriers inspire enduring fear and respect. The former, a physical sensation, is named figuratively; the latter, a twelve-foot-high reality, is named literally. They are both named 'the wall.'

"One of the clearest memories I have from Pensacola is of the brief moment when I paused atop the wall for the last time. Miraculously, I had made it to the top. Looking ahead at the rest of the course, I knew that the only thing between me and the finish was a few minutes of gut-straining exertion. I could handle it and, in a flush of relief, I knew that there was nothing insurmountable between me and my wings . . ."

Altitude chamber and water survival training are examples of strenuous, physically demanding training activities which are covered first in the classroom

AOCS students are not always so clean and pressed. Described by AOCS alumni as one experience that is actually fun—of sorts—this frolic in the mud is intended to convey the message that nothing is so bad it can't be survived. USN

and only afterward in action. Hours of instruction precede each phase of practical work. The Navy's idea is not only that the candidate knows what to do but why.

Water survival training

It can't be said too strongly that water survival is essential to the naval aviator's life from the earliest days and throughout a career. For the student naval aviator who continues onward, AOCS water survival training at Pensacola is just the beginning. Every four years, naval aviators and aircrew must renew their certification in aviation physiology. This refresher training includes aspects of high-altitude flight, general ejection seat requirements *and* water survival.

The water survival school is the largest department in the Naval Aviation Schools Command at Pen-

sacola in terms of staff personnel. The Aviation Physiology Training Unit (APTU) syllabus includes swim training, deep water environment survival training (DWEST), land survival and physical training.

In the pool

Part of the water survival training is conducted in a large swimming pool with devices to simulate situations aircrew might face after ejecting from their aircraft or ditching their helicopter.

The in-pool phase of training takes a full day. Students spend the morning in the classroom reviewing the physiological aspects of flying—the effects and symptoms of hypoxia, drugs and colds. After a light lunch, the students don flight gear and assemble at the pool. APTU maintains a rack of old flight suits, g-suits, harnesses, helmets and boots for use in water survival training.

The classes are normally ten to twenty people and are conducted by specially trained swimming and survival instructors, normally mid-level enlisted personnel. Officers are the flight surgeons who administer the APTU and who are ultimately responsible for the quality of training.

The training pool at Pensacola, where candidates are dunked, learn water survival and practice an abandon-ship drill, is one place where officers and instructors are exceedingly serious. AOCS' leaders want to be very certain that all of their instruction is safe. AOCS training, however demanding, is in fact very safe indeed.

The in-pool curriculum starts with a seventy-five-yard swim—three pool lengths—in full flight gear, a much more grueling exercise than it looks, followed by drown-proofing and an examination of methods for surviving in the water after ejection.

The next part of in-pool training is less strenuous and a little more fun—but still more difficult than it first would appear. The students practice pulling themselves into one- and multi-person rafts that are floating in the pool. The skittishness of the rafts and the extra weight of their sodden flight gear makes this challenging for even the strongest students, but with the instructors' guidance and a few strategically placed straps, the students soon get the hang of it.

Following the raft phase, the students receive training in helicopter hoisting and being dragged by their parachutes. The helo hoist is an assembly which realistically simulates the student dropping into the water and being covered by his chute's canopy, a potentially hazardous situation. Entanglement in their canopy and chute riser straps has killed many aircrew after an otherwise safe ejection.

Officer cadets are sometimes called on to serve as honor guards for previous classes' graduation ceremonies. USN

36

AOCS students select flight suits to wear during water survival training. USN

The class assembles at poolside to start their 75–yard swim, about three pool lengths, in full flight gear. One of the instructors is already in the water. Peter B. Mersky

Three students try their hands at entering a large life raft. Even in the placid confines of a pool, entry is not easy. In rough seas, the task would be considerably more difficult. The students always wear their helmets, and are directed to do so in an actual survival situation. The helmet's reflec-tive tape helps locate survivors, especially in the dark or in heavy seas. Thus, if the aviator removes his helmet, or loses it, he decreases his chances of being seen from a rescue helicopter. Peter B. Mersky

A student is hoisted above the pool and dropped into the water. Then his chute canopy settles down on top of him creating a potentially dangerous situation. Following a normal ejection and safe water entry, many aircrewmen have become entangled in their chute's canopy and riser straps. Some have drowned. Knowing how to extricate oneself from the entanglement is an important part of the survival training. Peter B. Mersky

The helo hoist simulates being lifted into a rescue helicopter amidst the spray of the helo's downwash. Peter B. Mersky

A student drops into the pool to begin the parachute drag portion of the training. Once he enters the water, the straps will pull him along the water's surface, simulating being dragged by a partially-inflated parachute. Peter B. Mersky

After freeing themselves from their chutes, the students paddle toward the helo hoist, connect themselves to the hook and are lifted out of the water amidst a disorienting spray created by pipes. This mist simulates the water kicked up by a helicopter's downwash.

In a real ejection and parachute drop the canopy may still be filled with air, and as it settles onto the water, any wind may catch in the chute, dragging the hapless aviator along. The chute might also fill with water and sink, dragging the crewmember to certain death. Thus, it is vitally important that crew members know how to right themselves on the surface while being dragged and release themselves from the chute as quickly as possible.

To teach this the APTU uses a device called the "slide." The student perches on a platform with an instructor. After connecting to the harness, the student is dragged from the platform—about 10 feet off the water—and as he is pulled the length of the pool, he must flip himself onto his back and reach the Koch harness fittings just below his shoulders to release himself from his chute. Again, this is much more difficult than it seems, but vitally important to learn because an aviator could quickly drown if dragged through rough sea.

The final phase of in-pool training is three to five dunks in one or both of the underwater egress trainers.

The largest of the two, the 9-D-5, is known as the helo dunker. Looking like an oversize garbage can, the helo dunker simulates the middle fuselage of a large helicopter like the SH-3A or multi-place aircraft like the E-2C Hawkeye. It is open at the hatches and windows.

With a load of students the helo dunker is winched above the pool and dropped to simulate a ditching. Its cabin quickly fills with water and it sinks. Now the students must find their way out of the dunker, under water, in reduced light. To make this even more difficult, the dunker can be turned upside-down to simulate the helicopter rolling over, a very real possibility, especially in heavy seas. This training is important, even for nonaviators, such as VIPs and ship's company personnel who travel between ship by chopper. They can experience a ditching even though they are within sight of their ships.

The other dunker the students may have to endure is the 9-U-44 single-place underwater egress trainer. Since World War II, this trainer has been known as the Dilbert dunker, after a cartoon character created by John Osborn of *Grampaw Pettibone*

The 9–D–5 helo dunker suspended from the overhead. Peter
B. Mersky

The 9–D–5 hits the water and begins to rotate, simulating a ditched helicopter's rolling over. Helicopters are naturally top-heavy since their rotor blades and engines are mounted atop the fuselage. In heavy seas, a helo can roll over and trap its occupants. Training with the helo dunker helps aircrewmen find their way out of such a situation. Peter B. Mersky

Students also practice using their flight helmets as flotation devices. USN

fame. The Dilbert dunker teaches underwater escape from a single-place aircraft such as the A–4E Skyhawk or F–18 Hornet.

The student is strapped into the metal car. The instructor throws the switch, and the car slides down a rail into the pool, flips over and sinks. Disoriented and quickly running out of breath in the dark, submerged "cockpit" of the trainer, the student must fight back panic while unstrapping and swimming to freedom.

Though it was once a part of all AOCS students' training, the Dilbert dunker, for the most part, has been relegated to retirement—not because it is dangerous, but because it is difficult and expensive to maintain. And a study is underway to decide whether to dismantle the remaining Dilbert dunkers.

Dunker training is one of the most dreaded aspects of AOCS and AI. But most find out that it is not as dangerous or terrifying as they thought it would be. A naval flight officer describes his dunker experiences: "I didn't think the Dilbert dunker was that scary, I thought it was easy. I never thought it was as bad as the helo dunker. [Helos] don't have a lot of accidents but if they do have an accident, it's the most critical aircraft to get out of when harnessed. It's like a big garbage can. They drop it down and it floats for a second and then they rotate it 180 degrees so you're upside down. It's kind of scary."

But it would never be as scary as the scene in *An Officer and a Gentleman* where the student becomes disoriented after riding the dunker into the pool and almost drowns. The scene shows the Marine DI diving into the pool to rescue the student while the enlisted pool instructors stood by. "That couldn't happen," says the NFO. "They have professional divers that watch you. They have tanks. They have oxygen supplies and these are professionals and they would not ever let it get that far."

By the end of the day, no matter how great their physical conditioning, the students are completely drained and happy to see the end of the class.

Offshore

Other water survival training is conducted out-of-doors offshore from Pensacola. AOCS candidates and AI students go through this training separately, as do numerous other Navy personnel. Students practice descent and disentanglement from a parachute and coping at sea with helicopter rotor downwash. Perhaps the most exciting (and wettest) part of the training is a simulated open-water parachute descent using a parasail pulled by a tow boat.

At the end of the training sessions, students take a breather in their soaked flight gear, happy for the chance to stop and exchange stories and viewpoints. Peter B. Mersky

While the US Navy's water survival program, particularly at Pensacola, occasionally shows up in gaudy headlines because of mishaps involving students, the truth is that the training program saves hundreds of lives, ensuring that naval aviators know what to do when real-life ejections and ditchings inevitably occur.

Peer rating

During the tenth week of AOCS, you receive a peer rating. Each candidate nominates the top three and bottom three members of the class. A point is awarded when you're mentioned on top and a point subtracted each time your name appears on the bottom. Students at the bottom are not washed out solely because of these ratings, but the ratings usually accurately reflect a trainee's overall performance.

These peer ratings, combined with the grades received on drills and inspections and the evaluation of each candidate by the DI and class officer, are used

next page
In the open-water phase of training, the students practice setting off flares. Flares are used by downed flyers to make their location more visible to rescue crews. Rob Ketchell

to assign candidate officer ranks for Applied Leadership Week. That's the last week of AOCS, when candidates are placed in responsible positions to carry out duties of the battalions and the training of new classes.

The Navy's welcome booklet warns, "If you make a mistake or fail to follow a regulation, you are usually given demerits and assigned EMI (extra military instruction). This time is worked off either by extra drill practice or by doing chores such as cutting grass or painting. You are not permitted to leave the base until your EMI is worked off."

Ensign bars

For the hard-earned and all-important moment when AOCS ends and candidates are commissioned as naval officers, a dress ceremony is held and family members are invited. For the candidates, it is time to be pinned with the gold bar of an ensign (and incur an obligation to serve as an officer in some other capacity if flight training is not successful). For the Navcads, it is time for the next step on the road to a commission. An all-important decision about "what next" is made at this juncture.

Water survival training includes a trip out to sea in this boat.

Midshipman Cindy Mason prepares to pull down the face curtain that will launch the ejection seat up the track of the ejection seat trainer. USN

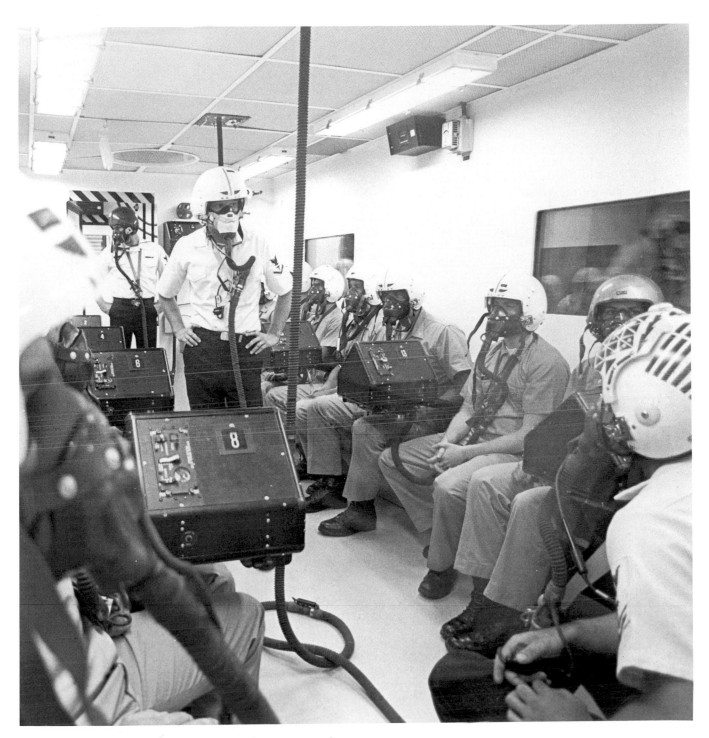

Midshipmen wearing flight helmets and oxygen masks prepare to undergo high-altitude flight testing in a hyperbaric chamber. USN

During an inspection, a battalion officer checks an AOCS candidate's white uniform. In addition to Marine drill instructors, AOCS students are overseen by career naval aviators. USN

This is when the intelligence and maintenance officers head off to pursue their specialties. The men and women who will fly also now fall into two groups—student naval aviators and student naval flight officers. Those training to be Navy pilots will report to NAS Whiting Field at nearby Milton, Florida, or to NAS Corpus Christi, Texas, for primary flight training in the Beech T-34C aircraft. Student naval flight officers report to Sherman Field at Pensacola for basic and specialized NFO training.

Navy tradition requires a new naval officer to give a dollar to the first person who gives a salute to him or her. AOCS tradition requires that person to be the drill sergeant. Joe Fives, the future flier introduced in the previous chapter, must return a salute and pay out to DI Sergeant Crankshaw. Crankshaw donates his new dollars to charity.

Fourteen weeks earlier, when it looked like just getting through Poopie Week was a near-impossible challenge, the DI faced the group and accented the positive. "I assure you everything for the next fourteen weeks can be achieved if you have the right positive mental attitude and a little motivation. At the end of fourteen weeks, I want to be able to salute you and call you, sir."

Now it has happened, and the next step toward becoming a Navy flier will actually put the student in a real airplane.

In The Pipeline
By ENS Mark Hutchins

The steps have been small and the difficult part definitely lies ahead but I'm on the way toward getting selected for the A-6 *Intruder* community. I finished the Aviation Indoctrination (AI) just before going on Christmas leave.

I was in a student pool for two weeks awaiting a slot for AI. A group of ensigns and 2nd lieutenants gathered at morning roll call each day. Some were assigned duties; some not. As the jobs are announced the whole pool listens in silence, everyone hoping they aren't "volunteered." Most of us ended up with some free time but it got boring real quick. It did give me and my roommate, another NFO candidate, time to settle into our condominium on Perdido Key, a 15 minute drive from the back gate at NAS Pensacola. We have a great location, 75 yards from the Gulf of Mexico. We step off our porch onto the beach. And I'm here till spring! The weather in Pen-

sacola in winter is nothing to complain about when you're from Maine.

Rumors, stories, tidbits of information—some of it erroneous—abound at AI. It all comes under the heading of "gouge"—that is, hints on what to study, how to answer questions, etc. There's a good spirit here. We try to help each other out. Students come from extremely varied backgrounds. A French major may sit next to an aeronautical engineering graduate. In the long run, its still up to the individual to make it, however.

A main topic of conversation focuses on the future, what lies ahead, how hard its going to be. Although academics is the key in AI, there is PFT—physical fitness training, which includes the obstacle course, swim tests and the like. In PFT, you either pass or fail. Few have trouble with this part. You're given extra time and work if you need it, same as with

previous page
To mark graduation from AOCS, those being honored appear on the parade ground in full dress whites, including sword. Candidates in khaki uniforms are still in training in AOCS and, after some attrition, will graduate at a future time. Rob Ketchell

The moment every AOCS candidate waits for—to have AOCS behind. As part of being commissioned ensigns in the Navy, candidate graduates stand in formation in front of the presenting stand where they wait until their name is called, then proceed up for a ceremonial handshake and salute. Actual graduation takes place in Pensacola's Naval Aviation Memorial chapel across the street. Rob Ketchell

Having just received her first salute from her Marine Corps drill instructor, this newly-commissioned ensign and AOCS graduate now receives congratulations. USN

academics. Some people feel your standing in academics is more important than anything else down the line.

The material is straightforward. If you concentrate, work hard at absorbing the instruction and read the questions on the test properly, it helps. Class averages on tests are normally in the 90 to 95 percent range. Make a few careless mistakes and your class ranking suffers considerably. The competition to excel, by the way, is great.

Unlike college, there are no skipped classes here. Staying attentive in class is a must. We take it seriously. After all, we are getting paid to learn. A lot different than paying to learn in college.

The temptation to go out and goof around is there but not too tough to overcome. Those that do that tend to drop out of the program early on.

I'm happy that I finished in the top quarter of the class but am also disappointed because I know I could have done better. Anyway, I'm anxious to start VT-10. I like to think that as I get closer to wings, the work will get better. I also know it will be more difficult. But nobody said it would be easy.

First printed in Wings of Gold, *Spring 1989*

Chapter 3

Primary Flight Training

With AOCS completed, our commissioned officer or Navcad is now ready for that first chance to actually fly an aircraft. So, too, are those who earned their commissions via routes other than AOCS and who have completed aviation indoctrination at Pensacola.

At this point, many who wanted to become pilots learn that they cannot meet the requirement for 20/20 vision in both eyes with adequate peripheral vision. One or two may decide to DOR (drop on request). Most, however, will choose to become naval flight officers (NFOs), whom we will meet next in chapter 5.

For the SNA (student naval aviator) or pilot trainee, the first taste of flying comes with primary flight training in the Beech T–34C Turbo Mentor, or "Tormentor" as some will call it. The training program will also include a considerable amount of "flying" in a ground simulator, with civilian employees performing the instruction.

The Beech T–34C Turbo Mentor training aircraft costs about half as much to fly as its predecessor, the North American T–28 Trojan. When the T–34C first appeared in the late 1970s, it drew some criticism because of costs and delays, but it has subsequently proven to be a safe and successful aircraft.

The T–34C is powered by a Pratt & Whitney PT6A–25 gas-coupled turboprop engine, making it the first turboprop to be used from primary training. The engine drives a three-blade Hartzell hydraulic propeller. This powerplant has operating characteristics similar to the jet engines used in the very latest fighter and attack aircraft.

The engine is offset to the right and down from the aircraft centerline to cancel much of the torque effect from the propeller. This enhances the jet-like feel of the T–34C. Engine and airplane are remarkably quiet, the overall noise level less than any other trainer. Although the engine is capable of 715 shp (shaft horsepower), the Navy restricts maximum power to 400 shp by incorporating a torque limiter. At a gross weight of 4,300 pounds, this reduced power satisfies all performance requirements demanded in the training environment.

The Navy tells us that primary flight training lasts 17.6 weeks. This includes fourteen flights (21.8 hours) of familiarization or FAM, eight flights (13.0 hours) of basic instrument (BI), six flights (11.0 hours) of radio instruments (RI), five flights (7.6 hours) of precision landings and aerobatics (PA), six flights (10.4 hours) of formation flying (Form), and two flights (2.6 hours) of night familiarization (NF).

Also included in primary is 39.5 hours of simulator and 101.5 hours of academic class time. Engineering and meteorology make up the bulk of academic work but also included are communications, instrument navigation, aviation student information (ASI), flight rules and regulations, and—not surprisingly—aerodynamics.

According to Frank Bachman, a simulator instructor at Corpus Christi, the three skills most needed by the student pilot are motivation, the ability to concentrate and personal organization. The last is probably most important. "You have to have organized work habits or there's no chance of learning the rest of it."

Primary flight training is at one of the four training squadrons. These are VT-2 "Doer Birds," VT-3 "Red Knights" and VT-6 "Sixers" at NAS Whiting Field in Milton, Florida, and VT-27 "Boomers" at NAS Corpus Christi, Texas. All are equipped with the T-34C and with T-34C simulators.

Before actually flying, SNAs go through a familiarization course in the cockpit of a mock-up T-34C. This way, the student learns the position of the throttle, rudder pedals, landing gear handle, fuel gauge and other instruments vital to aircraft in flight.

Student pilots discover at primary that flying is not simply a matter of kicking the tires and taking off. There is the continuing demand for attention to detail. For example, there are eight distinct steps in preflighting the relatively simple T-34C. In those eight steps are no fewer than eighty-one specific points the student must check from memory, to the instructor's satisfaction.

Then the student pilot takes to the air. After about twelve flights with their instructors, together with strenuous work in the simulator and many hours of briefings, SNAs are ready for the next of many major hurdles which lie between them and their wings of gold—flying solo. Taking off, putting the T-34C through its paces, and landing it while entirely alone is one of those milestones of a lifetime—an experience not easily forgotten.

In the civilian world, instructors make a special effort to surprise students when it's time for that all-important first solo. One of the authors made his first solo after an instructor pretended to see something odd outside the aircraft, stepped out, then slammed the door and cried, "Go ahead! Get out of here!"

In the Navy, this doesn't happen. Give or take a moment or two, every student knows exactly when he or she will solo the T-34C—usually after ten hours and fifteen minutes of dual instruction. The surprise is left out, but the event is a thrill nevertheless.

You never just go up and fly. Every quarter-hour of every flight has a prescribed instructional purpose. Every aspect of the flight training plan is written down in books the student is well-advised to memorize.

The student pilot in the T-34C now speaks a new jargon. "Fams" are familiarization flights, those first trips aloft in the aircraft. One youngster made it all the way through AOCS, passed the rigid eyesight requirements for pilot training, then became airsick

Primary flight training is taken at NAS Whiting Field, Florida (shown here) or at NAS Corpus Christi, Texas. These student naval aviators are passing the operations building at Whiting Field. The airfield, which has three T-34C squadrons and two helicopter training squadrons, is possibly the busiest in the world. USN/JOC Kirby Harrison

previous page
Pretty as a picture in the Texas sun at Corpus Christi, the Beech T–34C Turbo Mentor, the "Tormentor," is the Navy's primary trainer and will remain so for at least the remainder of the century. This one belongs to squadron VT–27, called the "Boomers." Robert F. Dorr

during initial Fams in the T-34C. That's why primary is called "puke school." Surprisingly, the airsick student may not have to DOR (drop on request) giving up a lifetime dream of flying. Aviation medical experts have concluded that for a great many students, airsickness is psychologically induced by tension and/or anticipation. Those with apparent chronic airsickness are now sent for evaluation and treatment, and many return to complete their primary training.

A few students will find that, despite years of preparation, handling stick and rudder is not for them. A few very fine young people discover, contrary to what they had thought, that piloting an aircraft is a disturbing experience. Let's face it: the act of propelling a tube of metal through the open air is not a natural experience. No shame need be associated with the conclusion that flying is not your piece of cake.

The student struggles to avoid getting a "down"—that is, a decision by the instructor that a flight in the

Before he can fly the T-34C, the primary flight student must first "fly" the ground simulator, properly known as a Cockpit Procedural Trainer (CPT). In the simulator, the student learns all about instrument flying by using realistic flight controls and an instrument panel with real dials and gauges, telling him such things as speed, altitude, and heading. Here, a civilian instructor (right) prepares a student for a simulator "flight." Rob Ketchell

Student naval aviator performs pre-flight check on Beech T–34C Turbo Mentor. The student must check 81 specific points on the T–34 before each flight. Peter B. Mersky

A formation of Beech T–34C Turbo Mentor primary trainers over NAS Whiting Field. Formation flying is a difficult skill to master and the first formation flights demand complete concentration from the students. Peter B. Mersky

T–34C or the simulator didn't count because of failed performance. A down will put a pink sheet in your folder, reason for worry. If you get a down, you get two ETs (extra times)—two chances to make up the failure. Two downs and you meet a PRB (progress review board). Three downs will wash the student out of the program. Like AOCS and AI, the primary flight phase has an attrition rate. It is typically around sixteen percent.

By the time student pilots complete their eighteen weeks of primary, they will have accumulated about sixty-five hours of actual flight time, ideally three flights a week. They will have satisfactorily demonstrated a mastery of takeoffs, close-formation flying, aerobatics and precision landings. They will have a thorough knowledge of instrumentation, navigation and communications. They also will have shown an ability to deal with simulated emergencies.

Toward completion of primary flight training in the T–34C, the student pilot is approaching that all-important decision on what lies ahead. Once primary is behind, a decision will have to be made which

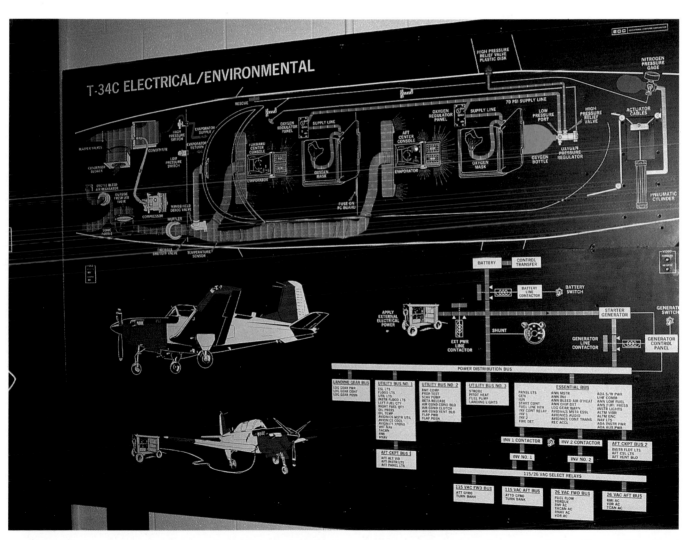

The T–34C is purposely a simple aircraft, but even the most rudimentary airplane can require a tremendous amount of "booklearning." Students must, for example, memorize the electrical and environmental details on this chart, which cover but one aspect of the aircraft. Rob Ketchell

determines which of three pipelines the student will go into—strike (meaning fighter and attack aircraft), maritime (meaning multi-engine, propeller-driven craft) or helicopter.

Some students ask for maritime or helicopter training because they really prefer it for a Navy career. Helicopters in particular really do attract enthusiasts who have never wanted to fly anything else—although unlike Army helicopter pilots, they have now gotten fixed-wing experience in the T–34C. Other students in what some call the "me" generation, seek multi-engine training out of a very practical interest in the airline job market after completing Navy service.

Exact figures do not exist but the obvious remains accurate. More than helicopters, more than multi-engine aircraft, student naval aviators want to enter the strike syllabus in order to fly fighter or attack jets. And among those who want to fly jets, most want to fly fighters—the F–14 Tomcat or F–18 Hornet.

Each class of student naval aviators has this decision made on the basis of several factors. First and foremost comes the need of the Navy. If the Navy has a severe shortage of helicopter pilots, everyone in primary may be sent over to Whiting Field for helo training. Second and decidedly less important, comes a student's preference. The top-graded student in primary may (the key word here is "may") get his first choice. This is likely to be strike but not always.

So we have come to a juncture. On completion of primary training, our future Navy pilots will separate. For most of them, at least two major stages of additional training lie ahead before winning those coveted wings of gold.

Student and instructor prepare to go aloft in a T–34C. At first, even though prepped for the airplane by time spent in the simulator, the student will be limited to learning the basics of flight such as the operation of controls and flight surfaces, and landing and taking off. As training progresses, the student will fly actual instrument hops and learn more about both visual and instrument flying while in the front seat of the T–34C. Rob Ketchell

Chapter 4

Intermediate Strike

Some say it should be a museum piece. Included are British Aerospace people at Dunsfold and Douglas people at Long Beach. But it's not a museum piece yet. Five squadrons use it. It doesn't get much recognition, the short and fat Buckeye. Those who fly it, like it. Depending on whether they want to go into fighters or attack aircraft, they call it the "Air Superiority Buckeye" (a shoulder patch) or the "Attack Guppy."

It's not pretty. It isn't graceful. But the North American T-2C Buckeye jet trainer wearing the white and red-orange paint scheme of Navy trainers is a striking sight—and never more than when a south Texas electrical storm is brewing in the distance and the mostly white T-2C reflects the glare of sunshine while black, billowing storm clouds churn in the background.

The SNA (student naval aviator) who has reached intermediate strike in the T-2C knows that the dreaded detour has not happened; the SNA has not been channeled into the multi-engine or helicopter pipelines. The dream is still alive. The Buckeye is midway between the primary T-34C and the advanced TA-4J on the fast-jet path. Succeed in the Buckeye and you may end up flying those Tomcats or Intruders.

Neither the student nor, for that matter, the instructor, is likely to know a great deal about the history of the Buckeye trainer. Those flying the aircraft are younger than it is. There are some Buckeyes in museums, including all the surviving T-2A models.

Built in Columbus, Ohio, to meet a 1956 requirement, the two-seater tandem trainer was named for the Buckeye State. The Buckeye made use of familiar components. Its wing was derived from a postwar, straight-wing jet fighter, the FJ-1 Fury. The control system was adopted from the veteran T-28C Trojan. The T-2A version was powered by a single 3,400-pound thrust Westinghouse J34-WE-36 turbojet engine.

The first of six preproduction T2J-1 (YT-2A) Buckeyes flew at Columbus on 31 January 1958 piloted by veteran Richard Wenzell. Buckeye deliveries to the US Navy began in July 1959. A total of 217 T-2As were built. Two examples were modified to become service-test YT-2B prototypes, powered by two 3,000-pound thrust Pratt & Whitney J60-P-6 turbojets. Following an initial flight on 30 August 1962, ninety-seven T-2Bs were built.

The final American version of the Buckeye was the T-2C which introduced two 2,950-pound thrust General Electric J85-GE-4 turbojets; 231 were built for the Navy. The T-2C remains the standard for pilot training until it can be supplanted, then replaced, by the British Aerospace/Douglas T-45A Goshawk, which is also slated to replace the TA-4J Skyhawk as the Navy's advanced trainer.

The T-2C is capable of 521 mph at 25,000 feet, has a service ceiling of 44,400 feet and has the advantage of single-point refueling. The able civilian contractors who maintain today's T-2C fleet are often asked how the US Navy can keep flying an aircraft originally planned to have a service life of around ten years which now is well into its fourth decade. Expected service life of the T-2C has been extended from 4,800 to 12,000 hours making it necessary to repair wing spar cracks. In the late 1980s, the T-2C was experiencing a higher than acceptable wing spar failure rate. By the early 1990s, these failures are expected to affect ninety percent of the T-2Cs in the fleet. The Navy is developing Operational Safety Improvement Program (OSIP) kits to address the problem.

This middle phase of jet pilot training is carried out by three squadrons, the "Green Frogs" of VT-19 at McCain Field, NAS Meridian, Mississippi; the "Professionals" of VT-23 at NAS Kingsville, Texas; and the "Tigers" of VT-26 at Chase Field, NAS Beeville, Texas. An additional outfit, the "Warbucks" of VT-4 at Pensacola, Florida, provides both intermediate T-2C and advanced TA-4J training. The earlier T-2B model of the Buckeye is still in use with the "Cosmic Cats" of VT-10 at Pensacola who train naval flight officers.

The authors looked at intermediate strike at Kingsville. South Texas—you step off the airliner at Corpus and the heat slaps you in the face. Heading south on narrow, sparse Highway 77, fully one-third of the radio stations on the dial are in Spanish. At McDonald's a guy asks, "Habla espanol?" and orders his Big Mac in Spanish. This is storm country, tornado country; but 335 days out of 365 yield CAVU (ceiling and visibility unlimited) flying weather. And there's nothing to run into down here, not so much as a molehill, for the land is as flat as a board. Instructors complain that young pilots leave here knowing nothing of mountains, valleys or canyons.

One of the squadrons offering T-2C jet training is VT-23 "Professionals" at Kingsville, Texas. Marine 2LT Marshall Denney, a student naval aviator, poses in front of building *which removes any doubt about squadron nickname.* Robert F. Dorr

The North American T-2C Buckeye trainer used for intermediate strike at Kingsville, Beeville and Meridian. Aircraft 158900 with commodore's 300 side number belongs to VT-21 "Professionals" at Kingsville. USN

Student pilot suiting up for T-2C jet flight at Meridian. Their G-suits and helmets are individually tailored. A student always wears this greenish one-piece flying suit, called a Poopie Suit. An instructor may, if he wishes, wear a blue flight suit instead. Rob Ketchell

The newly-arriving SNA soon learns that Kingsville, twenty-nine miles south of Corpus Christi, is a big and friendly town, a tourist town because of the famous King Ranch. Naval aviation is welcome here, but the pressure of flying and booklearning will cut into any time earmarked for the town's one movie or its half-dozen beef cookeries. The pressure is everything.

Ensign Lance Norton (that's really his name) got his commission via the college ROTC route, took AI

Locker rooms and ready rooms are filled with flying safety reminders, one on the merit of wearing a visor to protect the eyes. Going to and from flights in the T–2C Buckeye, students must be thinking about "stick and rudder" skills but they must also ponder an encyclopedic volume of aviation data which they're expected to have memorized. Rob Ketchell

(aviation indoctrination) at Pensacola and went through five months of primary at Whiting Field before reaching VT-23 for the T-2C Buckeye phase. He hasn't been out to the carrier yet.

Norton says it can get frantic when a student makes a mistake in a T-2C maneuver. "The instructor gets upset. You have to do it over and over again." The student can, but shouldn't, get flustered. "Some days it snowballs. It gets so bad by the time you're in the landing pattern you can't even land." This condition is known in slang as helmetfire: "The student's mind gets so confused he doesn't know what he's doing." But, he says, "I try not to let the pressure bother me."

Another slang term is "gouge" which means—more or less—the real story, the inside scoop. "The instructor in a T-2C sits high enough, he can see if a student is reading the gouge from a knee clipboard." The gouge includes rote answers to technical questions, aircraft performance figures, anything the student is expected to rattle off by rote. The gouge is also known as the "juju."

The Buckeye has seen a lot of abuse over the years, adds instructor Denny Fitzgerald. "You can do anything wrong in one and still recover." But, Fitzgerald warns, a flustered student can "squeeze the black paint out of the handle" with a taut grip on the stick.

Flight syllabus

The first step in intermediate strike: the SNA is fitted with a new pair of "speed slacks," otherwise

While a civilian maintenance expert glances at the broken nose cone up front, student naval aviator pre-flights a *Meridian-based T-2C Buckeye in preparation for a flight.* Rob Ketchell

called a G-suit, and with nylon, velcro and steel torso harness intended to be carried into a full career of flying. Flight helmets are all fitted to the individual, and Navy SNAs are unable to avoid the lame joke that helmets worn by Marine SNAs are different: "Theirs are smaller."

Instructor and student don't simply go up and fly. Much of the SNA's time is spent with academic work, but when the flying does take place, it follows a rigid syllabus with precise requirements for every quarter-hour of the flying schedule. Intermediate strike is 22.8 weeks, including forty-five hours in the simulator and eighty-nine T-2C flight hours.

Before flying, the new intermediate strike student receives two weeks of ground school in air sys-tems, aerodynamics and instrument flight rules. Next, the simulator. And finally, the T-2C Buckeye for a series of "FAM" (familiarization) flights. Much later, the student will learn formation flying and carrier landing.

The skipper of the VT-23 squadron at Kingsville points out that virtually all landings in the T-2C are carrier landings. Having begun in the slower T-34C, the student now must get used to thinking at six miles per minute instead of two and one-half and not flaring over the runway end numbers.

Landings can be traumatic for the student who was impressed throughout primary training with the importance of gently touching the runway with the landing gear. Now the student is exhorted to collide

After performing the pre-flight check, a student taxis his T-2 Buckeye toward the runway. Rob Ketchell

with the ground by chasing an elusive light around on something they call a fresnel lens, a procedure called "flying the ball," and as if that isn't enough, to maintain a precisely calibrated air speed at the same time.

When you fly the ball you're watching the Fresnel lens and adjusting the descent of your aircraft. Depending on what happens to the lens—whether it moves up or down, left or right—you can tell that you're above or below glide slope or to the left or right of the center line. If you fly the ball until your tailhook catches the number three wire, you've made a perfect landing.

At Kingsville, the student practices carrier-style landings and flies the ball on every landing. A mock carrier deck replete with four wires for the T-2C tailhook is located out amidst great expanses of nothingness at Orange Grove, Texas. Intermediate strike trainees make ten arrested landings with an instructor who is a qualified LSO (landing signal officer). Once the student gets out to *Lady Lex* in the T-2C, the student makes two touch-and-gos and four arrested landings. Later on, if the student advances to the TA-4J Skyhawk, there'll be two more go-arounds and six arrested landings.

Most students come to the T-2C expecting to be rigorously judged on their stick and rudder talents. They are, but it can't be emphasized enough how much the prospective naval aviator must study during the T-2C phase. A brain-twisting document called the Master Curriculum Guide contains 129 pages and must be memorized by rote. Even something as simple as the formation flying instructions for the T-2C occupies sixty-four pages and too must be memorized.

In discussing T-2C training, it is worth saying again that we cannot use the male gender for all SNAs. In today's integrated Navy, women are reaching the intermediate strike syllabus and can go on to fast jets. Rosemary Mariner, one of those in the first group of female naval aviators (1973) was in the multi-engine pipeline and got orders to a Grumman S-2 Tracker squadron. Later, Mariner came to Kingsville for the jet transition syllabus, went through the T-2C and TA-4J phases, and is now carrier qualified. Mariner then became XO (executive officer) of electronic warfare squadron VAQ-34 at NAS Point Mugu, California, fly-

Even when aloft, as on this student solo flight at Meridian, the T-2C is not exactly beautiful, but its guppy-like profile evokes affection from those who fly the aircraft. Rob Ketchell

69

At various stages in training, students get a welcome change from athletics. This boxing match took place during the intermediate strike phase, between two students. Peter B. Mersky

ing the Vought EA-7L Corsair II. The law still prohibits women from participating in combat, so even though Mariner can take an A-7 aboard a carrier, she cannot serve in a carrier air wing or live aboard ship.

In our visit to VT-23, we saw a number of female students and instructors. Ensign Pam Lyons is a Sergrad, something no student at Kingsville wants to become. A Sergrad is a selectively retained graduate—a student who was kept after graduation and made into an instructor. The only advantage to this purgatory is that after Sergrad duty, you can get just about any aircraft assignment you want. Among T-2C students is Ensign Nancy Davison, who came into the Navy with an advanced degree in biomedical engineering and wants to be an astronaut. Times have changed since the late 1970s when recruiters found it difficult to sign up capable people. Today's student naval aviators are the *crème de la crème*. Twenty percent of T-2C students are Marines, who have a somewhat different philosophy—a young officer in the Corps does not have as much responsibility piled

As in primary flight training, precision formation flying is one of the most important and most difficult aspects of intermediate strike. The students in the rear two T-2Cs practice flying formation with an instructor in the lead Buckeye over NAS Kingsville. USN

on immediately as a Navy counterpart—and who do not have to worry about becoming Sergrads.

The VT-23 skipper says his T-2C phase is intended to pass along three abilities to the student: a good instrument scan, good headwork in the cockpit, and carrier landings. Anyone who doesn't know about an instrument scan should consider a principle taught in ACM (air combat maneuvering) sessions: "lose sight, lose the fight." When you're twisting and turning with a simulated opponent you must keep

Note the sturdy tailhook under the tail of this T-2C. It is used nearly every time the students land in the Buckeye— *whether on the practice field at Kingsville or on the* Lady Lex. USN

These students fly their T-2Cs out to sea for CQ (carrier qualification) practice on the USS Lexington. *Even after* hundreds of *"traps," or arrested landings, a carrier landing is never routine.* Peter B. Mersky

your eyes on him—but the T-2C, like the TA-4J and some combat aircraft, lacks a head-up display so the student must learn to quickly size up his instruments without losing that mock MiG.

It might be suspected that carrier operations are the ultimate in the T-2C phase of training, and indeed they are. Navy people attach a mystique to carrier landings and with good reason; possibly no other act in aviation is such a test of sheer flying skill. While pilots understate this sort of thing, the truth is that a carrier landing requires utter fearlessness. When the SNA is cleared to take the Buckeye "on the boat," a juncture is reached where some students, even after faring well to this point, decide to DOR (drop on request). Most, of course, succeed in landing the Buckeye on the *Lexington* and being launched from the ship. *Lady Lex*, which has been the Navy's training

carrier since 1962, is too small and lightly crewed to accommodate aircraft, so T-2Cs and TA-4Js are not allowed to RON (rest overnight) aboard the carrier.

All training flights to the carrier are made in daytime. The aviator does not experience night operations until reaching a fleet readiness squadron in the aircraft he'll fly in service. Night landings, even at such a late date, also produce some dropouts.

After carrier landings, catapult shots and air combat maneuvering, the student naval aviator is finished with intermediate strike and, finally, with the T-2C Buckeye. Next comes advanced strike in the TA-4J Skyhawk and, after that, the wings of gold which transform students into rated pilots. Most will look back at the Buckeye with what one calls a "warm, fuzzy feeling," regarding the T-2C as user-friendly and pleasant to fly.

Chapter 5

Naval Flight Officer

Does anyone choose voluntarily to undergo months of drill, of pressure-cooker training, of constant struggle with physical, academic and aeronautical challenges, knowing all the while that success—attained only with the greatest of difficulty—will bring a slot in the *back* seat of an F-14 Tomcat or a navigator or electronic warfare slot in a larger aircraft? Does anyone seek to be a crew member rather than a pilot? Who are those guys?

It is said that the best naval flight officer (NFO), rather than having the freewheeling, high-flying instincts of a pilot, is the tinkerer, the gadget freak, the young Tom Swift who played with computers and tried to build a time machine in the basement. NFOs, if they're good, have a special rapport with machinery and electronics. It is not easy, bending over a scope in a Hawkeye or Tomcat or seated, windowless, in an Orion or Viking trying to make things happen with somebody else in the driver's seat.

The Navy claims not to know how many NFOs choose this career field from the beginning. A few do. It appeals to some that in an F-14, for example, the back-seater has a key role in navigating, locating and identifying targets, and plotting the air-to-air engagement—even firing the missiles sometimes. So a few students start out hoping to be NFOs.

The NFO is at least as important to the Navy as the pilot, maybe more. The list of job slots is long. An NFO may become a navigator on a long-range patrol aircraft such as the P-3C Orion antisubmarine plane, an airborne tactical data systems officer on an E-2C Hawkeye airborne warning and control aircraft, a bombardier/navigator on the A-6E Intruder attack

jet, or a radar intercept officer in the back seat of an F-14 Tomcat. About the only place an NFO won't end up is in a rotary-wing aircraft; helicopter crews do not have NFOs.

Naval aviators—pilots, that is—may think themselves more important even if all they do is drive, but

AOCS graduate and future naval flight officer (NFO) Joe Fives poses with Pensacola sign which reveals squadron VT-10's nickname. Joseph H. Fives

73

the Navy assigns equal importance to the NFO and gives the NFO equal chances for promotion and command.

The truth, though, is that most don't choose from the outset to become an NFO. The wings of gold worn by the NFO signify opportunity and a potentially rewarding career for the young person who is highly competitive but who can't meet the eyesight requirements to be a pilot.

Again, our focus is on Pensacola, where the first naval air station was established in 1914 and where Captain W. I. Chambers obtained and flew the first Navy aircraft. From biplanes to the Blue Angels, this city is inextricably linked with the Pensacola air station and its half-dozen outlying installations.

The city of Pensacola also has lovely beaches along the Gulf of Mexico, a historic district centered on Sevilla Square and a much-loved basketball team called the Tornados. Young men and women learning to fly for the Navy are warmly welcomed in this historic city—but they're unlikely to have much time during training to enjoy it.

Our future NFO has completed AOCS or, if already commissioned via other means, has completed AI (aviation indoctrination), so Pensacola is becoming familiar by now. That training in AOCS or

Before their first flights in the T–34C, student NFOs must learn how to quickly and safely get out of the Mentor if it becomes necessary to parachute or ditch. This emergency egress trainer was made from the remains of a salvaged T–34. USN

AI marked the first and last time that our future NFO will be getting the same instruction in the same place as the future pilot.

SNFOs (student naval flight officers) will have ahead of them a long and winding trail with intense and varied training. But it all begins at Pensacola with the basic NFO curriculum.

Cosmic Cats

The first step after AOCS or AI is to remain at Pensacola where the "Cosmic Cats" of squadron VT-10 offer basic and intermediate NFO training. Remaining at Pensacola does have one advantage: student NFOs who are married can now be joined by their spouses who become authorized dependents at Navy expense. Not a lot of leisure time will be available to enjoy family pursuits, however. Subjected to the stress of demanding academic and cockpit training which goes on throughout all phases of training, the student NFO will spend twenty-one weeks with VT-10, receiving 250 hours of academic study and twenty-five hours of flight time.

Basic NFO training

Before our future flier can do much flying, the first challenge is a basic NFO curriculum heavy in academic demands. Flight and academic courses are divided into basic and intermediate stages, with training in navigation, meteorology, flight physiology, safety, communications, and flight rules and regulations. Again, the Navy makes use of ground simulators which do not eat up costly aviation fuel, are far more economical than actual aircraft and serve pretty much the same purpose. The 1D23 navigation trainer and the 2F101 flight simulator provide twenty-five hours of hands-on preparation for the moment when flying does take place.

Student NFOs initially ride in the Beech T-34C Turbo Mentor, the same aircraft in which student pilots undergo primary training. The basic phase includes five sorties in the T-34C and one in the T-2B Buckeye twin-engine jet. Those who go on to the intermediate phase at Pensacola will again encounter the T-2B and, afterward, the T-47 Cessna Citation.

In The Pipeline

This is the third of periodic accounts from ENS Mark Hutchins who is based at NAS Pensacola where he is pursuing the gold wings of a Naval Flight Officer.

Its hard to believe that I am finally going to get up in the air. Its a relief to have completed ground school. We've been in "Basic" for two and a half months getting ready and still haven't been in a plane as compared to our pilot counterparts at Whiting Field. But just because we're NFOs doesn't mean we're not as excited about flying as the pilots. The first few flights in the T-34C may be a lot busier than I expected. I never imagined so much preparation was required before going up.

Ground school is book work and tests. Doing well at this doesn't necessarily mean you'll do well in the air. I've heard of some students who excel in ground school but can't handle the fast-paced, high pressure environment in the cockpit. I wonder a lot how I will do.

Once in flight stage, each student is responsible for his own schedule. Its a mystery to me how they manage that schedule. I do know that it comes out daily at 1700. If you ask a buddy to check it for you and he makes an error, its your neck on the chopping block, not his.

Although I've had rides in Navy planes before, when I go up this "first" time it won't be as an observer. I'm the one being observed—by the instructor. As they told us in ground school, the instructor is a voice-actuated autopilot. Instructors will fly wherever you tell them as long as it doesn't endanger the occupants.

Being able to tell the pilot to take you wherever you want to go may sound great to some. But here at VT-10 the instructor has the important function of evaluating your skills and grading the student NFO in a variety of categories. The student has to get an "up" before he continues in the program. Anything other than an up is bad news and means the student really needs some work. I often wonder how much of what we learn at VT-10 will have application in the fleet. I know that briefings, checklists and reports are part of activities in a fleet squadron, but perhaps to a different extent. I think the real idea here is to create a high pressure environment for the student, to see if he or she can hack it. Even though I haven't been up yet I know the workload in the T-34 will be pretty good. Even if you do everything perfect, you would still be busy 100 percent of the time. You're nervous, you're bound to make mistakes, and things don't happen exactly as we were taught in ground school. You probably wish there were more seconds in each minute and more minutes in each hour.

We all have a picture of what its going to be like in the air but we don't have the experience of how all those things we have been taught fit together. I guess nobody is perfect. You just do the best you can and don't allow the instructor's yelling to bother you too much. I'm just hoping that I make the right calls, get the basic format down, demonstrate sound knowledge of everything, and come out of in as good standing as everybody else.

Looking ahead, we have two graded simulators flights and five basic flights in the T–34. After the fifth, we graduate from the Basic stage. At that point students will break off into the jet or prop pipelines. Lately we've been hearing that about 85 percent of the students get their first choice. About two-thirds of each class (generally, there are 30 students per class) will go on to Intermediate VT–10 for jet train-ing, while the remaining one-third will go to Mather AFB California for instruction in propeller type aircraft.

I'm hoping for jets. I want A–6s. I believe the *Intruder* promises excitement and fun. There's a lot of talk about the A–6 and how it is aging. All I know is that I am very impressed with the A 6 mission and believe I could perform well in that type of environment.

To tell the truth, even though training command time seems to be flying by, selection for jets and finally getting winged seems a long, long way away. There's a lot of work ahead but I know for sure that I would much rather be doing this than anything else.
First printed in Wings of Gold, *Summer 1989*

Maritime NFOs

After basic NFO training, students who have been picked for maritime patrol or electronic surveil-lance—meaning that they'll serve aboard P–3C Orion patrol aircraft or the EP–3 Orion electronic surveil-lance version—depart Pensacola. They cross the country to take the twenty-two week interservice undergraduate navigator training (IUNT) program at

The F tailcode and distinctive checkerboard design on the rudder are the markings of VT–10, alias the "Cosmic Cats," the Pensacola squadron which trains future naval flight officers in the North American T–2B Buckeye. Peter B. Mersky

Mather Air Force Base near Sacramento, California. Some years ago, the government decided to train all long-range navigators in the same place and assigned the task to the Air Force.

The Air Force aircraft employed in the IUNT program is the T-43A, a version of the twin-engine Boeing 737 airliner. It's the largest aircraft used to train Navy fliers. Each T-43A has no fewer than nineteen stations—twelve for navigation students, four for proficiency training and three for instructors.

The IUNT curriculum includes 345 classroom, eighty flight hours and seventy-eight simulator hours of training. On completing the IUNT program, student NFOs receive their wings and orders to their first fleet squadron.

next page
Those student NFOs destined to become long-range, over-water navigators split away from their cohorts and proceed to Mather Air Force Base near Sacramento, California, where they learn their profession in the Air Force's T-43 trainer, a military version of the Boeing 737. Doug Remington

Some naval flight officers will go into the airborne tactical data systems (ATDS) pipeline and will report to the east or west coast fleet replenishment squadron (FRS) for the E-2C

Hawkeye airborne early warning aircraft. Fifteen weeks at the FRS will prepare a newly-commissioned NFO to join the Fleet. USN

Intermediate NFO training

Meanwhile, future NFOs who did not peel off for the journey to Mather remain at Pensacola in VT-10's "Cosmic Cats" for the intermediate phase of NFO training. Afterward, they'll be heading in different directions depending on what aircraft they'll crew in actual service.

During this intermediate phase of NFO training, students accumulate forty flight hours, ten in the T-34C, 11.7 in the T-2B, and 18.3 in the T-47A. No relief from academic pressures is offered, however, and students must still undergo 103 hours of classroom study.

T-47

Even its manufacturer readily admits that the Cessna T-47A is not the prettiest airplane in Navy inventory. In fact, the Navy wanted to call it the Platypus but the nickname didn't stick so the craft is better known by the same name given civil executive jet versions, namely Citation II.

Fifteen T-47As are operated at Pensacola under a "package" arrangement which includes maintenance and simulator support, replacing North American T-39D Sabreliners which trained SNFOs for many years. Unlike its business jet counterpart, the T-47A has nose-mounted Emerson APQ-159 radar and an airframe which has been strengthened for high-speed operations at low altitude and for extended life in high maneuvering and turbulent flight conditions.

The T-47A is powered by two 2,900-pound thrust Pratt & Whitney Canada JT15D-5 turbojet engines and has a maximum operating speed of 358 knots. The aircraft has a single pilot (a civilian contract employee) and a student occupies the right cockpit seat. Normal crew is pilot, a Navy/Marine Corps instructor, and two or three flight students. The Cessna T-47A routinely flies a 300-knot profile at 500 feet above ground and is often subjected to 4 Gs when acting out the role of a fighter in a modified air combat maneuvering environment.

The whole object of NFO training, of course, is to make training as realistic as possible. Ugly and uncomfortable it may be, but the T-47A is the ideal

The Cessna T–47A Citation jet is employed for intermediate naval flight officer training. The Navy nicknamed the aircraft Platypus, having in mind the odd shape with the nose radar installation, but no one uses the name. Stephen H. Miller

aircraft for simulating some of the larger airplane types operated by the Navy. At the same time, it is relatively inexpensive to operate and small enough that the instruction provided has a personal touch.

As this volume went to press, the T-47 contract was replaced by a contract with Sabreliner Corporation. Intermediate NFO training will now be performed in Sabreliner aircraft.

During the training of naval flight officers, some specialized training is given to Marine Corps student NFOs who will fly the Corps' two-seat F-18D Hornet. The Marines are relinquishing their fleet of A-6 Intruders in order to procure increased numbers of F-18Ds, and will use the Hornets in the attack and reconnaissance roles—missions not performed by Navy Hornets. In this sidelight to the larger syllabus, the Marine student NFO gets flying experience under conditions similar to those of actual attack and reconnaissance flying.

Advanced tactical data systems

The student NFO group is constantly undergoing change with the arrival of new faces and departure of the familiar. Following basic NFO training with VT-10, another group peels off. Departing now are students who will specialize in airborne tactical data systems (ATDS). They will be officer crew members aboard the Grumman E-2C Hawkeye, the twin-turboprop, early warning aircraft with a disc-like rotodome above its fuselage. It's not an easy task, overseeing the radar and electronics work of the E-2C—warning the fleet of any impending attack—and the Hawkeye does not get much publicity. More attention should be given to the simple fact that E-2Cs, by far the biggest airplanes to operate from carrier decks, land and take off on their surveillance missions dozens of times a day with remarkably few mishaps. E-2C people are a proud community and, with or without rave notices, they know that their mission counts.

In The Pipeline
By ENS Mark Hutchins

This is the fourth of periodic accounts from ENS Mark Hutchins who is based at NAS Pensacola where he is pursuing the gold wings of a Naval Flight Officer.

Well, here's more from the Pensacola, the land of white beaches. In my last report I wrote about my expectations with respect to how much fun and how busy the flying would be. I finally got in the air. It has been a great experience but even in the T-34C I would emphasize the "busy" over the "fun."

I completed the *Mentor* syllabus in June and graduated from basic stage. I lucked out when it came to selection for future duty and got jets as I had hoped. A number of guys didn't and were disappointed. Our class was somewhat unusual in that all but a few wanted the jet pipeline. There was bound to be some frustration. You just can't predict what will happen.

From the moment I started the program I looked forward to flying in the jets. As I have discovered, however, the thrill and enjoyment of such flying has been immensely tempered by the responsibilities assigned during the hops.

Between giving the pilot headings, altitudes and airspeeds, handling the radios, figuring fuel data and time estimates, and completing all the checklists, I have been totally engrossed in the cockpit. There's not much enjoyment. I suppose this has to do with the fact that there are a limited number of syllabus hops in each aircraft. Just about the time you feel comfortable working in one plane, you're done flying it.

This makes sense because the thrust of our training entails the techniques of navigation, communication, etc. The basics are hammered into us and the more we master those the more comfortable we become in the air.

Performing well in the training command environment is dependent on your ability to stay relaxed and think clearly when a whole bunch of things come at you at once. Even if you are very well prepared for a given flight, things can go wrong. Radio reception might be poor, you may have to change your route of flight due to weather, any number of things. Because you are traveling at 360 knots over the ground you must make your adjustments quickly. You can't waste time making decisions.

As I write this I have two more T-2 *Buckeye* flights before moving on to T-47s at VT-10. I have liked the exposure to the different kinds of missions flown in the fleet. We have done some basic fighter maneuvers (BFM) in the T-2 and will do low-levels when we move on to the T-47 *Citation*.

Things are moving quickly. Those wings of gold don't seem nearly as far away as they used to.
First printed in Wings of Gold, *Fall 1989*

Our future NFOs for the E-2C Hawkeye pick up their sea lockers and proceed directly to east or west coast fleet readiness squadrons (FRS) operating the E-2C for fifteen weeks of advanced training in the aircraft. After this advanced phase, the ATDS group will receive NFO wings. But their aircraft is so complex, they'll have still a further fifteen weeks learning the on-board computers and radar and sensor systems of the E-2C. Only after that comes the Fleet.

Advanced NFO training

As our ranks thin out with the departure of two groups of future UNFOs, we have remaining at Pen-sacola those who will go into overwater jet navigation (OJN), tactical navigation (TN) and radar intercept (RI) work. All of these specialties involve operating from carriers. These future NFOs now proceed to advanced NFO training, still at Pensacola, with squadron VT-86.

Overwater jet and tactical navigation

This squadron operates TA-4J Skyhawks and T-47A Citations. Overwater jet navigation and tactical navigation students fly both types and receive instructions on how to navigate safely, using visual and airborne ground-mapping radar. Those studying

For the student NFOs that have reached advanced NFO training the dream is still very much alive. They will likely fly in either the A–6 Intruder as a bomber-navigator or in *the F–14 Tomcat as a radar intercept officer. The others will serve as overwater jet navigators in the S–3A Viking. USN*

to become tactical navigation officers concentrate on weapons, weapons delivery and electronic warfare. The TN specialty will get the student a slot on an A–6E Intruder or EA–6B Prowler. The OJN field is for future crew members of the Lockheed S–3A Viking carrier-based antisubmarine aircraft.

In The Pipeline

Ensign Hutchins is training to become a Naval Flight Officer and reports periodically to Wings of Gold *on his progress.*

In my last report I was flying T–2B *Buckeyes*. In VT–10 I also flew in the T–47 Cessna *Citation,*modified for NFO training purposes. The transition from the T–2 to the *Citation* entailed going from one radio, one TACAN and analog fuel gages (which, incidently, made figuring total fuel on board a bear!) to two radios, several nav aids, and a digital fuel totalizer readout.

At first our tasking seemed easy with all the "fancy" equipment. I learned quickly, however, that having extra equipment called for extra attention.

For the first time in the syllabus our instructor was someone other than the pilot. The pilots are civilians, the instructors "fleet" NFOs who can devote all of their attention to the student. Which is good *and* bad. Good, if you, the NFO student, know what you're doing. Bad, if you're not so sure. Overall, this close scrutiny makes learning the duties of an NFO much easier.

We flew Instrument Navigation (INAV) in the T–47 first, in order to become comfortable working in a crew-concept environment. After INAV we flew low-levels, undoubtedly the most exciting flying in the training command. Although dogfighting in the T–2s was exhilarating, the low-level flights were more rewarding. Whipping along at 300 knots, 500 feet above ground, over the VFR military training routes is a kick. The student's job is to direct the pilot with headings and airspeeds in order to reach the "target on top" within 30 seconds of planned TOT. It's a fast moving, stimulating environment down low and reaching the "bombs away" on top point, on time, is absolutely great!

This experience convinced me even more that I really want to be an A–6 *Intruder* BN.

After the low-levels and graduating from VT–10 I was most happy to be selected for the Tactical

---

Before the advanced student NFOs get to fly in the A–6, F–14 or S–3A, they will train in the TA–4J Skyhawk and T–47A Citation. This student NFO performs a visual check on the TA–4J before a flight. Rob Ketchell

Radar intercept officers

Our final group of Navy/Marine student NFOs is the group training to become radar intercept officers (RIOs). These are the real-life versions of *Top Gun*'s "Goose," aspiring to occupy the back seat of the F-14 Tomcat fighter. With squadron VT-86 they, too, train in the TA-4J Skyhawk and T-47A Citation and spend considerable time in the 15C4 ground radar trainer.

Flying at high-speed in a highly maneuverable tactical aircraft, being subjected to violent, high-G maneuvers as the pilot flings the craft about, is not for everyone. Some who want to become radar intercept officers find that being strapped tight inside a bucket of bolts while zigzagging through open space is simply not the right thing for them. Those student NFOs who are working to become radar intercept officers and who don't mind treatment akin to that of sardines in a can, press on in the back seat of the TA-4J Skyhawk, and learn how to conduct an air-to-air intercept of an unidentified or possible enemy aircraft.

The emphasis of their training is on functioning as a teammate with the pilot of a fighter while under the stress of high-G fighter maneuvers. After seventeen weeks of training which includes the inevitable high dosage of academic work, this student will receive wings of gold and will be posted to an F-14 Tomcat fleet readiness squadron before joining the Fleet.

Coast Guard NFOs

The Navy has long included sixty Coast Guard officers per year in its aviator training program. Now,

Those naval flight officers who will become bombardier-navigators in the Grumman A-6E Intruder have yet another aircraft to learn upon reaching the fleet replenishment squadron (FRS). The Grumman TC-4C, a version of the Gulfstream propliner, has been modified with the radar nose of an A-6E. Inside the TC-4C, future BNs learn how to use the A-6E radar and instruments. Grumman

the NFO training program is offered to Coast Guard officers who will man the service's E-2C Hawkeyes in the nation's antidrug effort. In setting up a special syllabus for these future fliers, due attention has been paid to the fact that Coast Guard fliers routinely fly in weather that grounds other aircraft, since that's when other people have emergencies at sea. The T-47A, which emphasizes radar procedures, is the key to this part of the program, followed in importance by the TA-4J where the flight training stresses crew coordination and visual lookout tactics.

Wings

The award ceremony where an NFO receives his or her wings is every bit as important, as poignant, as the "winging" of aviators. The occasion calls for dress whites, visits by family and introductions to senior officers and instructors. After the "winging," our future member of the Fleet will be able to enjoy the first vacation since leaving civilian life so long ago. Chapter 9 describes what happens next—when you reach the fleet replenishment squadron (FRS) which instructs in the airplane you'll fly in the Fleet.

In The Pipeline
By ENS Mark Hutchins

ENS Hutchins reports regularly to Wings of Gold *enroute to the gold wings of a naval aviator.*

Time is whipping by. I'm in VT-86, a tour which began with two weeks of concentrated ground school. We reviewed aircraft systems in the T-47 *Citation* and became familiar with the term, "front loaded." Basically, everything we were expected to do in VT-86 as a TN (tactical navigator), excluding the *Skyhawk* syllabus, was taught in the classroom in those first two weeks. Areas covered were airmanship, low level and radar planning and navigation, lowland and mountain predictions and crew coordination.

When it came time to begin the mountain radar hops weeks later, it was not easy going back and reviewing all that we had tried to comprehend in the classroom those first two weeks. But the demands of the syllabus dictated this "front loading."

I flew five low levels in the local area utilizing basic formulas for wind analysis and time and course corrections to navigate. We flew at 300 knots, 500 feet above ground to reach the target on top/on time, using only visual cues. Traveling that fast and that low does not allow time to pull over and study a map or ask for directions.

When not flying we worked on navigation charts and radar predictions. There were 20 charts, each requiring two to three hours to prepare. Even more time consuming were the radar predictions that would accompany the charts.

We had to develop a picture of the predicted radar returns and shadows using training paper placed over turning points and targets on the chart. By studying the natural and cultural features shown on the Tactical Pilotage Chart (TPC) and by comprehending the various types of returns created by these features, we created a picture close to what

would be observed on the actual radar scope. Each radar predictions took an hour to finish. All told, we had to prepare 70 radar predictions.

After the low levels, I "flew" radar navigation hops in the simulator. "Live" radar nav hops took place over routes similar to the earlier low levels.

Radar navigation procedures are very detailed but as I got more hops under my belt I was able to look at the 45 degree sector (on the nose) scanned by the radar and determine by location and time what each bright blip on the radar corresponded to on the chart.

I learned to correlate all the information on the scope to recognize turn points and targets. Of course, I fed this information to the pilot, directing him along the route to the target.

On the mountain radar flights, I learned to use cultural returns (factories, towns, bridges) as well as shadows created by mountain ridges to determine the aircraft's position.

I was elated when I passed my Tactical Navigator Checkflight and have since moved on to seven TA-4 *Skyhawk* flights which will lead to completion of the VT-86 syllabus and the ultimate goal: getting my wings.

At times I feel as if I've only learned the basics but we are told by the instructors that in the fleet we will find ourselves falling back on these basics.

I'm eagerly looking forward to the air combat maneuvering we'll be doing in the *Skyhawk*. Beyond that, I'm still hoping for orders to A-6 *Intruders* and ideally, a squadron on the east coast. The suspense is killing me!

By the way, I successfully got married on 30 December 1989. Everything's going great!
First printed in Wings of Gold, *Spring 1990*

Chapter 6

Multi-Engine

They call it the maritime pipeline. Some pilots who come out at the far end wearing wings of gold will spend their flying lives on long-range, over-water journeys in land-based aircraft, hunting for submarines or hauling cargo. Others will come and go from carrier decks in the biggest aircraft to operate aboard ship. All will look back at their training for Navy wings and think fondly of the conviviality of their cohorts and the sturdiness of the T-44, that twin-engine trainer some call the tank.

For years, Hollywood, the Pentagon and the recruiting corps have told us that most student pilots want to fly jet fighters. Statistics bear this out. But at Corpus Christi in those hot flatlands of south Texas where all multi-engine (maritime pipeline) training takes place, a surprising number of student naval aviators are in multi-engine training because they requested it.

Some go into multi-engine thinking candidly about a future of prestige and high income with the airlines. Our world is about to undergo dramatic changes which will mean unprecedented opportunity for those who seek an airline career after completing their service obligation, typically six years. Retirement of a generation of baby boomers will mean that those who leave the service in the period 1996–98 will face a wide-open job market. In fact, there will be a desperate shortage of airline pilots. One major airline by itself will need 2,000 pilots in the middle of the decade.

The Navy needs these pilots to stay in the Navy. In fact, some improvement has been achieved in pilot retention in recent years now that a career in uniform has become respectable again. Those who make the Navy a career will enjoy a special opportunity all their own. They'll move up to head the crew of a large aircraft many years earlier than they would with an airline. They'll have unprecedented chances for promotion and for early command.

Though the outflow of naval aviators to commercial carriers is still a flood rather than a trickle, most students who make it to multi-engine training are at least considering a Navy career and, if there by choice, have selected the maritime pipeline for some reason other than the airlines. Marine Corps 2LT Paul Gomez is tickled pink at the prospect of flying four-engine C–130s but remains concerned that, with frequent overnight stays away from his home base, the fighter jocks will dub him a "per diem cowboy."

Probably the strongest motive for multi-engine enthusiasm is also the simplest. Some people just plain don't want to live on the boat. An aircraft carrier takes its crew away from home for six to eight months at a time. Land-based multi-engine flying—overnight stops and all—permits the naval aviator to spend most of his time at home.

next page
Typical of large, multi-engine Navy aircraft which need both pilots and naval flight officers, the Lockheed P–3C Orion is a formidable, far-reaching patrol craft and the nemesis of Soviet submarines. Masumi Wada

The maritime pipeline—the Navy's term for the path to a multi-engine pilot's slot—begins with the sturdy Beech T–44 Pegasus, the Navy's trainer version of the civilian King Air. Students find that the T–44 does an excellent job of simulating the aircraft they'll fly later in their careers. Beech

Our multi-engine student aviators are the future pilots of Navy P–3C Orion antisubmarine aircraft and of Marine Corps C–130 Hercules tankers and cargo lifters. Receiving similar but not identical training are the future pilots of the C–2A Greyhound carrier onboard delivery (COD) transport and the E–2C Hawkeye airborne early-warning craft.

These student pilots got this far by going through AOCS or following another path to a commission, then passing primary and intermediate training in

Marine 2LT Paul Gomez is a student naval aviator who has reached the multi-engine phase and has graduated from the T–34C Turbo Mentor to the Beech T–44A (background).

Success in the multi-engine pipeline will make Gomez a pilot of a Marine C–130 Hercules. Robert F. Dorr

Many graduates of the multi-engine pipeline, including virtually all Marine graduates, will fly the four-engine Lockheed C–130 Hercules, the most successful transport of the turboprop era. This KC–130F Hercules tanker/transport is arriving at NAS Glenview, Illinois, near Chicago. USMC/Robert F. Dorr

One of the best multi-engine jobs in the Navy or Marine Corps is flying the Blue Angels flight demonstration team's C–130 Hercules support aircraft. Since the Angels perform around the world, the assignment obviously requires pilot and other crew members who do not mind travel. USN/PH2 Paul O' Mara

the T–34C Turbo Mentor. The Navy does not have a universal pilot training scheme like the Air Force's. In the Air Force, every pilot goes through the same training, concluding with advanced work in the T–38 Talon jet trainer; this is an almost useless experience for the future pilot of a C–141 Starlifter or C–5B Galaxy. As this volume was being prepared, the Air Force was planning for the first time in forty-odd years to adopt a new scheme similar to the Navy's wherein the pilot of a large tanker or transport would train in a multi-engine rather than an advanced jet aircraft. In the Navy, our multi-engine students, like all student naval aviators, receive specialized training. The maritime pipeline students will never have reason to strap into a T–2C Buckeye, TA–4J Skyhawk or any other jet aircraft.

At Corpus Christi are the "Rangers" of VT–28 and the "Wise Owls" of VT–31, the two squadrons which provide advanced multi-engine training in the T–44A, itself a twin-engine turboprop naval version of the popular Beechcraft C–90 King Air. The first T–44A was delivered to Training Command at Corpus on 5 April 1977 and student pilot training began in July 1977, the T–44A replacing TS–2 Tracker piston-engined airplanes.

T–44

It's sturdy all right, and solid. It might have come from an iron works. On the ground, moving from

Pilots destined for the E–2/C–2 community are the only student naval aviators who go through the maritime pipeline and receive carrier qualification training in the T–2C *Buckeye. The E–2 Hawkeye is better known than the Grumman C–2 Greyhound (shown) which is used as a carrier on-board delivery (COD) aircraft. USN*

The most apparent difference between the Hawkeye and the Greyhound is the Hawkeye's radome. E-2 and C-2 pilots are among the most skilled of tailhookers, landing these heavy aircraft on the deck of a carrier with very few mishaps. USN

The Lockheed P-3C Orion pilots are trained to endure long, overwater patrols that last many hours, patrolling for Soviet submarines. USN

"Rangers" of VT–28 are one of two squadrons which pro-vide multi-engine training at Corpus Christi, and the

"Turbodillo" is a south Texas animal resembling the twin-engine T–44. Robert F. Dorr

taxiway to runway, it's heavy and a little tight on the controls. The T-44 is a big plane, not lithe nor nimble. But aloft the tank-like characteristics vanish and it becomes a pleasure to fly. The power of its engines is impressive and the T-44—solid and safe on the ground—becomes a good performer once in the air. The T-44A is powered by two 750-shp Pratt & Whit-ney Canada PT-6A-34B turboprop engines. The T-44A can reach a maximum cruising speed of 222 knots (256 mph) and has a service ceiling of 21,800 feet. The T-44A carries a full set of instruments and its seven-place cabin is air-conditioned and pressurized.

The T-44 is said to have reliability of well over eighty percent. In multi-engine, working hours are consistent and long-range planning works. The T-44 community is able to plan ahead with confidence in a way other people in aviation can only envy.

The authors noted what seemed to be rather limited visibility with the pilots' seats sunken deeply below the narrow windshield, but instructors insisted that this was the same as the E-2C and other aircraft the students will fly with the Fleet.

The T-44 is fully instrumented with its navigational alphabet soup of dual VORs, Tacan, RNAV, ADF and weather radar which means that the student can

next page
The Navy's T–44 multi-engine trainer is another aircraft which never won any beauty contest, but it has proven highly practical and effective in service with Training Command since the late 1970s. The "D" tailcode, expressed as Delta, caused confusion with Delta Air Lines and has since been replaced with "G." Robert F. Dorr

In the intense classroom setting, student naval aviators learn everything from characteristics of their particular aircraft to instrument and navigation techniques. The teaching is fact-oriented and exerts strong pressure on the student to memorize by rote—so that in the air, when neces- *sary, action will come almost by second nature. Academic work, including the bookwork which occupies a student and instructor before and after a flight, never ceases to have importance even in the advanced multi-engine stage.*
Rob Ketchell

practice any method of flying expected to be carried out later, and a "failure mode selector box" enables the instructor to select any of ten equipment failures on the students' instrument panels.

Maritime syllabus

During this multi-engine phase, student naval aviators will complete 167 hours of academics covering meteorology, aerodynamics, flight rules and regulations, aircraft systems and navigation. Maritime students will also undergo twenty hours in the 2F129 full-motion flight simulator plus eighty-eight flying hours in the T-44. The maritime curriculum lasts about 130 days.

For the student, this is the first occasion when it becomes necessary to think about other people in the aircraft. Working in a big, multi-engine plane with another pilot, a navigator, and perhaps enlisted crew members, the student must acquire a new sense for teamwork. Students agree that the transition from a single-pilot cockpit into the world of dual-piloted aircraft requires a realignment of flying skills to include the skills of your copilot. Perhaps it is not just a superficial impression that multi-engine pilots (and students) are a little more gregarious, a little easier to talk with and know. Says the Navy, "The learning environment in the advanced squadrons is intention-

The blue flight suit is a dead giveaway that LT R. A. Rall is an instructor and not a student. Teaching multi-engine skills in the Beech T-44 is a challenge. Robert F. Dorr

ally more relaxed, making this transition easier for the student."

So it was not just our imagination. Multi-engine students really did seem just a little more laid back, a little more smug, than the Type A personalities heading into jets. There is a relaxed camaraderie in these training squadrons. One student, comparing multi-engine training with the earlier ordeal of AOCS, described T-44 training as being "like a normal life, like you're working on a master's degree."

The Navy is proud of the collegial atmosphere it associates with the multi-engine program. VT-28 and VT-31 have a reputation for providing a genial atmosphere in the wardroom—in short, for junior officer development.

In a typical year, VT-28 and VT-31 flew over 18,000 hours each. Each squadron has about forty officers and twenty-two enlisted people. The T-44

squadrons annually train about 400 aviators for the Navy, Marine Corps, Coast Guard and foreign air forces. Students and instructors can often schedule a cross-country training flight to some location where there is reason to go. A remarkable number learn cross-country work by flying to Andrews AFB, Maryland, for Homecoming Weekend at the Naval Academy in nearby Annapolis.

As with the other pathways that take the student to wings of gold, the maritime or multi-engine phase of training concludes with that all-important ceremony where wings of gold are pinned on. The new naval aviator will depart Corpus Christi not only with wings of gold but with an uncommonly rich assortment of friends who are likely to remain friends for a lifetime. From Corpus, the student's next stop is a Hawkeye, Greyhound, Orion or Hercules squadron.

Chapter 7

Helicopter

Most people at South Whiting Field don't look up upon hearing the *thwack-thwack* of helicopter rotors and the faint hum of the gas turbine engines. The sound is too commonplace. The two squadrons which provide all rotary wing training for the Navy, HT-8 and HT-18, have been pushing those red-orange/white helicopters, or helos as they are called in the Navy, through the skies for so long, with such inexorable predictability, even something which elsewhere would arouse a lot of interest—*any* helicopter—scarcely rates a twist of the neck.

HT-8 and HT-18 provide rotary wing training with the Bell TH-57C Sea Ranger, the Navy's fully instrumented version of the proven and versatile Jet Ranger.

Since everything in the Navy gets counted, the squadrons can even tell us how many "operations" (in this instance, the term refers to any of three events—a takeoff, landing or low approach) are carried out by the ever-busy helicopters. In the year before this volume went to press, no fewer than 1,176,729 operations were carried out by TH-57Cs at South Whiting and at six Outlying Landing Fields (OLFs) nearby. Five hundred helicopter flights per day, adding up to a thousand flight hours daily, would not be unusual—with a helicopter taking off or landing once every nineteen seconds!

Intermediate helo

Future naval aviators in the rotary wing pipeline get their first taste of helicopter flying when they arrive at HT-8 to begin the intermediate phase. They will have logged about 120 hours in the Beech T-34C during primary training but most will never before have ridden in a helicopter.

The Navy believes in specialized flight training, but has not yet emulated the Army, which begins rotary wing students on rotary wing aircraft and does not provide primary fixed-wing training like that in the T-34C to future helicopter pilots.

At HT-8, the students learn the intricacies of smoothly manipulating helicopter flight controls that require constant motion of both hands and both feet to make the aircraft respond in the desired manner. It starts out easy enough, moving the TH-57C in forward flight, but it becomes far more difficult to the newcomer when other flight regimes are introduced—like flying with "zero" air speed or even backwards. Helicopter flying demands skillful, coordinated use of all the flight controls coupled with visual cues from outside the helicopter.

The student is introduced to collective and cyclic pitch controls as new instruments of flight. As compared with a fixed-wing airplane, a rotor replaces the fixed wing as a means of creating lift, and the helicopter's hovering ability makes it possible for the craft to hover at "zero" speed. Experts say that rotary wing flying requires a different "sense" for the situation, a new kind of eye-hand coordination.

Early in the intermediate phase at HT-8, student pilots are taught to hover—and few find it easy. It requires all the techniques learned in fixed-wing primary training plus a few new ones necessary for precision motionless, sideward and backward flight.

As CDR Howard Wheeler, a helicopter pilot, describes it:

"From the time they sat you in the helicopter for your first flight until you're able to hover can take fifteen hours. The Jet Ranger of today is a great improvement over the old TH–13 of the 1960s which had laminated hickory rotor blades! The old TH–13 had a very sensitive center of gravity so that when you flew solo you had to bring a sandbag with you, a fifty-pounder, just to balance things! In those old ships, you had the added problem of having to manually control rotor rpm with the throttle, a task no longer taught and no longer needed.

"Working up to learning to hover, the student practices maintaining altitude, speed and direction.

You learn that all Navy helicopters hover while leaning slightly down and to the left because of the location of the tail rotor.

"Learning to hover, there's a high level of frustration and all of a sudden—whammo!—the frustration just drops off and it all comes together. You work up to this from the point where you're given the controls. At first, when you get the helicopter into a ten- or fifteen-foot hover, you sort of warble around and you do too much scanning—you scan the instruments for altitude and rpm, and you glance outside. All of a sudden, it comes: you need to look straight ahead, pick some place out there, a tree, a building, something you can see—and whammo! After that, you know how to hover."

The Navy and Marine Corps operate a variety of helicopters from carriers, surface warships and shore bases and have a continuing need for well-trained helo pilots. This

Sikorsky SH–3A belongs to the headquarters unit at the Atsugi, Japan, naval air station. Toshiki Kudo

103

The Navy is within a couple of percentage points of having more rotary-wing than fixed-wing aviators, and a variety of helicopters with diverse missions await the successful student helo pilot. One example is the Kaman SH–2 Seasprite used for light anti-submarine operations. USN

Both the Navy and Marine Corps operate versions of the tandem-rotor Boeing Vertol CH–46 Sea Knight, a familiar sight in the Fleet dating to the Vietnam era. Learning to fly a helicopter such as this requires a whole new set of reflexes and a new kind of thinking. DoD

Sikorsky SH–3G Sea King, used for carrier anti-submarine operations, is another Navy helicopter the future naval aviator may fly with the Fleet. USN

As the students' skill and confidence levels increase, more difficult maneuvers are introduced to develop the techniques needed to perform missions and handle in-flight emergencies. Teamwork is vital: the copilot concept is strongly supported in all phases of helicopter training, because teamwork is necessary to react quickly and correctly to many situations where the pilot at the controls does not always have a free hand to carry out many of the procedures.

Advanced helo

After some six weeks, a first solo and forty flight hours at HT-8, students move on to the advanced rotary wing phase at HT-18 where they must learn instrument flying skills in the TH-57C.

Simulator work

The simulator, first encountered by the future Navy pilot in primary, continues to be important throughout the rotary-wing phase. Before a student is allowed to fly basic instruments in a helicopter, five full-motion simulator hops must be completed. Basic instrument (BI) and radio instrument (RI) work is taught rigorously just as it is in intermediate fixed-wing training. The student must, in essence, learn to use cues on the simulator's instrument panel to get the helicopter from Point A to Point B without looking at landmarks visible on the ground.

Instrument flying, in the simulator and later in the actual helicopter, can mean stomach-wrenching stress. In the simulator, you're unable to have eye contact with the all-seeing, all-knowing civilian instructor. That instructor may seem your friend at coffee time, but while overseeing your flight in the simulator he's a gentle tyrant. He inserts problems into the instrument readings. He introduces changes in the "feel" of flying. With the multiple-axis movement of the simulator, you can experience vertigo. You can also get a clammy sensation of being boxed up, so you overreact when the instructor does introduce a simulated flight problem.

Once in awhile, simulator work identifies a problem with the student. One cadet was just not suited for flying and would come out of the simulator with welted, mottled red hands from putting a "death grip" on the flight controls. The Navy makes every effort to

The Bell TH-57C is the standard rotary wing trainer operated by both of the Navy's training squadrons at NAS Whiting Field, Florida. The chopper is similar to the civilian JetRanger and the Army's OH-58 Kiowa. Al Mongeon

"save" a candidate who has a chance. In this instance, the cadet washed out.

Cross-country

Nine additional simulator flights must be completed successfully by the student before a genuine, instrument cross-country flight takes place. The longest and most difficult part of the helicopter syllabus— even more challenging than landing on shipboard— the cross-country flight phase demands excellent basic instrument skills plus the ability to correctly interpret instruments and charts and respond to ground controller instructions. On completing the radio instrument phase, the student receives an FAA (Federal Aviation Administration) standard instrument card. Practical experience follows with six cross-country navigation hops in the TH–57C to cement this knowledge.

It's important to remember that in the Fleet, helicopters don't land only on strong, sturdy airfields or even only on aircraft carriers; the future helicopter pilot will have to land and take off from frigates, destroyers and cruisers. The ship's deck may be swaying or riding crests in the sea. The weather may be awful. But poor weather flying is not a part of the rotary-wing syllabus, just as it is not taught in intermediate strike or multi-engine. The Navy believes that

As in all other routes to Navy wings, student pilots in the helo pipeline have to endure many hours of intensive study for every hour of flight time. Rob Ketchell

Helos are as complicated as most fixed wing aircraft and the aspiring helo pilots at NAS Whiting are required to perform a thorough pre-flight check of their craft before each flight. Peter B. Mersky

After the pre-flight check, the student straps in and prepares to take off. Peter B. Mersky

Under the watchful eye of the instructor, this student brings his Sea Ranger down next to the tower, practicing smooth controlled landings. Peter B. Mersky

After many practice landings on the simulated helo pads at NAS Whiting the students get to practice small-deck landings on the HLT. The HLT trains the student to operate safely from the small, moving and bobbing helicopter pads on US Navy ships. ENS Susan Haeg/*Helicopter Safety*

In this photo, a student in a TH–57C makes a starboard approach on the HLT, following signals from the LSE (landing signalman, enlisted). ENS Susan Haeg/*Helicopter Safety*

its pilots should learn how to fly in good weather and acquire poor weather experience after receiving their wings.

Small-deck landings

Simulated small-deck landings are practiced as students prepare for their deck landing qualifications on the Navy's prototype Helicopter Landing Trainer (HLT) or IX–514. Back in 1985, the Navy decided that because helicopters have expanding at-sea operational missions and capabilities, the practice of using the carrier USS *Lexington* (AVT-16) as an undergraduate pilot helicopter carrier qualification platform was neither cost-effective nor suitable for small-deck training. The HLT, which has been operational since 1987, is a small ship, a shallow-draft, self-propelled vessel with a landing platform on its stern. It's superb as a rehearsal version of the real Fleet warships that pilots will land on in their operational careers.

With this first exposure to an actual ship at sea, the student must demonstrate to the instructor a consistent ability to land safely on a small moving deck. After that ability has been demonstrated, each student joins the exclusive club of shipboard qualified aviators. In fixed-wing aviation, the comparable experience would be the first carrier landing in the T–2C Buckeye. All naval aviators wear the same wings of gold but, unlike those in multi-engine flying, Navy helicopter pilots can take pride in being shipboard qualified, not merely on carriers but also on a variety of warships having provision for helicopters.

Helo tactics

At our next juncture in the helicopter syllabus, Navy and Marine students separate, one of the few occasions anywhere in the training program where these two kinds of future naval aviator are taught differently. A portion of training unique to the Navy teaches low-level, overwater basic instrument flying necessary for night operations, IFR search and rescue missions, and antisubmarine warfare. The Marine-unique portion concentrates on formation and low-level navigation hops and tactical approaches.

For Navy trainees, this final part of the TH–57C helicopter syllabus consists of helicopter tactics. Since helicopters in the Fleet are employed for a wide variety of missions ranging from search and rescue (SAR) to antisubmarine warfare (ASW), this instruction in tactics provides the student a brief exposure to many mission requirements expected of fleet helicopter pilots. Included are low-level day and night contour navigation, external load operations, confined area operations, night landing zone work and formation flying.

Once finished, the student will have spent a total of six weeks in HT-8 and twelve weeks in HT-18, with a total of over 200 hours of fixed-wing and helicopter flight time logged. It is time now for the traditional "winging" ceremony which will transform student into naval aviator. Ahead lies the final stage of training when the new aviator meets his or her aircraft type at a rotary-wing Fleet Replenishment Squadron. After that, it's off to the Fleet.

Chapter 8

Advanced Strike

Until you've watched those red-orange and white Skyhawks follow their own smoke-strewn trails around the south Texas airfield on a sunbaked, 100-degree day, you don't know just how busy a training field can be. It's not for nothing that jet training is located in flat, remote, hot places like Beeville, Texas, a town so small its cinema has only two screens or, as one jokester alleges, the local Baskin-Robbins has only one flavor.

Why flat, remote and hot? You need flat because students learning to fly jets can wait until later to learn how to fly in mountains. You need remote so student pilots will be kept apart from other air traffic. And it's hot in Beeville because all flat, remote airfields with good flying weather are hotter than blazes. So, too, is El Centro, California, where the TA-4J squadrons deploy for weapons work.

Busy? How about *hundreds* of sorties in a single day? That's not unusual for a training base.

Kingsville and Meridian are the other two locations where the advanced strike syllabus is taught in the TA-4J. Students slotted to fly aircraft in the strike community (A-6, A-7, AV-8B, F-14, F-18 or S-3A) come to advanced strike after completing primary in the T-34C and intermediate in the T-2C.

The TA-4J Skyhawk syllabus includes sweptwing familiarization, all-weather instrument flights, formation, tactics, operational navigation, advanced air-to-air and air-to-ground weaponry, air combat maneuvering (ACM) carried out against an experienced pilot in another TA-4J, and carrier qualification (CQ). In the TA-4J Skyhawk, students receive

eighty-six flights with 270 flight hours (including eighteen of ACM) and six carrier landings, all in a period of twenty-eight weeks leading up to being "winged" as a naval aviator.

At Kingsville, in a nook too small to call a classroom behind the ready room of the VT-21 "Fighting Redhawks," instructor LT Pete (Revo) Reeves readies student naval aviator Mark Milberry for a flight called an Airnav 10 Check. The two men have a cordial relationship and both seem in control, yet tension is in the room, tight enough to crack. Mark is expected to rattle off, by rote, answers to more than a hundred questions Revo might ask.

Their aircraft is the two-seat tandem trainer TA-4J, based upon the bantam A-4 (originally A4D) Skyhawk. The A-4 was designed by Douglas' Edward Heinemann in the mid-1950s when the Navy needed a small, lightweight single-seater able to carry a centerline atomic bomb on one-way missions deep into the Soviet Union. That mission was never realistic but in Vietnam the Skyhawk—so small it's the only carrier-based jet without folding wings—racked up an admirable tally of successes in Navy and Marine combat operations.

To student pilot Mark Milberry, the TA-4J is a friend but an unforgiving friend, as is instructor Reeves. Either will be stern with him if he makes a mistake. During their preflight conversation, Reeves looks at how his student filed his flight plan. Much research has gone into the jet log, a card on the kneeboard where facts are scribbled, but Revo warns Mark to use map charts to navigate, not jet logs. "Use the chart to punch data into the computer." There is also a discussion about the correct way to fold a chart.

"We'll go up to forty-five percent power. Head-knockers up. We disconnect external power. When taxiing out, you do the nonmandatory items . . .

"For takeoff, you run up the power, check things, roll. Approaching eighty knots it'll be, 'You have the airplane.' Rotate, set ten degrees AOA [angle of attack] and let it fly itself off. Climb out at 250 knots to nine thousand [feet]. Then hold it at 230 knots and talk to approach control."

Instructor warns student that if descending or approaching too fast, he can "dirty her up." The TA–4J has retractable speed brakes, referred to as boards. "You put the boards out. If it's still not right, you go into your missed approach procedure. You go into MRT [military rated thrust], pull the boards in, clean her up, no more than twenty degrees nose up."

LCDR Sandy Jones, operations officer of VT–24 "Bobcats" at NAS Beeville, Texas, checks out the nosewheel of a TA–4J Skyhawk advanced jet trainer. Robert F. Dorr

Again talking about how to make an approach, Revo cautions the student to approach at 180 to 200 knots. "Don't go down to 180 because you don't want the slats out at this point." The TA-4J has leading-edge slats which, when extended, increase wing area and drag for low-speed performance. They work on a principle so simple it's incredible: they have no battery or motor or wires; they simply hang loose when the aircraft is flying slowly. At just about 180 knots, the air rushing over the wing is strong enough to make them retract.

The discussion includes slang and salty rhetoric. If Mark descends too fast, warns Revo, he'll be "coming down like a big turd off a tall moose's ass." When an instructor becomes impatient, he may "pimp" a student (remind him of something, as in, "Boy, you need to get some power on").

The TA-4J

Our two-seat TA-4J Skyhawk trainer—except for five A-4E single-seaters flown by instructors at Meridian—is the final version of the Skyhawk to operate from Navy carriers. Its history is straightforward. The TA-4J trainer began operations with squadrons VT-21 and VT-22 at NAS Kingsville in 1969 (at a time when single-seat attack Skyhawks were acquitting themselves in combat in Vietnam) and came to Bee-

The Marine pilot named on the canopy rail of this TA-4J Skyhawk at NAS Meridian, Mississippi, had to be a high achiever to become instructor of the year with the "Eagles" *of VT-7. The sameness of TA-4Js lined up behind him are an illustration of how much competition there was. Rob Ketchell*

ville in the 1970s. It was a quantum leap over the TF-9J Cougar which it replaced.

The TA-4J is powered by a Pratt & Whitney J52-P-6 or P-8 turbojet engine which develops 8,500 to 9,300 pounds of thrust and pushes it through the air at speeds up to 620 mph at 20,000 feet. The ejection seats are rocket-propelled Escapac 1C-3 or 1F-3 models capable of causing a successful bailout even at zero speed and zero altitude. The 20mm M39 cannon carries 200 rounds and the aircraft has partial provi-

sion for ordnance, including tiny training bombs which look like tiny specks when dropped from a diving Skyhawk. Student naval aviators are especially challenged during their gunnery and bomb work in the TA-4J at the Training Command's El Centro detachment.

Tactical training

Instructor Reeves describes the student's move from the intermediate T-2C Buckeye to the advanced TA-4J: "Tactical training is what makes advanced

Midshipman Cindy Mason (center) and Lt. Mary Jorgenson (left) walk to the flightline for a demonstration flight in the TA-4. USN

*Lt. Jorgenson points out the rear seat cockpit controls to
Midshipman Cindy Mason.* USN

*Lt. Jorgenson signals from the cockpit of the TA–4 that she is
ready to begin her flight.* USN

strike different from the earlier phases of travel. The student is going to get into this Skyhawk and fly it the same way he'll fly an operational aircraft in the fleet.

"We start out by putting the student under the bag in the back seat, qualifying for the instrument ticket which permits him or her to fly in the airways. After instrument training, your student sits up in the front office of the TA-4J and wrings it out.

"Up to now, the future aviator has flown only the T-2C which has twin engines hanging down real low. This [the TA-4J] is the first exposure to a jet with its thrust on the centerline, which is a lot harder to fly. And the TA-4J has enough power to give you a real kick in the backside." Reeves points out that it's more difficult to "fly the ball" with the TA-4J, harder generally to bring the TA-4J aboard a carrier, and above all terribly challenging because the Skyhawk has a kind of "hairtrigger response" to the student's touch on the controls.

Like every student who has reached the advanced strike, Mark has gone through AI, primary (in the T-34C Mentor) and intermediate (T-2C Buckeye)

Getting off the ground. Being soloed by a student naval aviator with no one in the back seat, a TA-4J Skyhawk springs into the air from NAS Kingsville, Texas. USN

training. He now has flown the TA-4J "under the bag"—that is, in a simulated instrument condition with a hood over his head enabling him to see nothing but the panel in front of him. Now for the first time, Mark will be up front, able to see out of the TA-4J.

So begins yet another of the seemingly uncountable training flights in the TA-4J Skyhawk, made by a student lured to the jet pipeline by the sheer physical challenge of handling a high-performance aircraft in the tactical carrier environment. Yes, it remains true that the most commonly stated preference is for jet training, but not even the student who asks for it always realizes that this choice means being in training at least another year and a few months more than his buddies in multi-engine, E-2/C-2 or rotary wing training.

Advanced strike syllabus

We have already described what happens to this student in the intermediate phase, flying the T-2C Buckeye. Going into the advanced phase, the student gets another two weeks of ground school, logs several more hours of simulator time and begins those backseat, under-the-bag takeoffs in the TA-4J Skyhawk before moving to the front cockpit. Because the student has already mastered the basic skills of flying, the familiarization and formation stages in the TA-4J phase are brief and the student moves quickly on to pragmatic tactical air training.

In the weapons phase, carried out by the TA-4J Skyhawk in a Training Command detachment at NAS El Centro, California, students learn to place bombs, rockets and bullets on a ground target. In other stages they learn to navigate at low altitudes and high speeds and receive ACM (air combat maneuvering) instruction to teach them to maneuver through nearly every conceivable attitude in defensive, offensive and multiplane situations. Only after all this does the student reinforce that hard-earned status as a tailhooker by returning to *Lexington* for six more carrier landings and launches.

Wings

In all, our jet pilot has been through about eighteen months and 270 flight hours by the time he or she dusts off a dress uniform and stands in ceremony to

next pages
A TA-4J Skyhawk shoots a landing at Meridian. Making a touch and go, putting down on the runway and lifting off again, is not difficult but provides excellent practice for airfield pattern work. Rob Ketchell

After a hard day of flying, instructor and student walk back to the equipment room to complete the post-flight paperwork. Rob Ketchell

receive those wings of gold. If not impressed into Training Command as a Sergrad, the student then will go to one of the FRS squadrons for the F-14 Tomcat, F-18 Hornet, A-6 Intruder, EA-6B Prowler, A-7 Corsair or S-3 Viking.

This former student, now a full-fledged naval aviator, has been through one of the longest and most complex training regimes of any civil or military flying organization in the world, at any time in history. He (or she) has seen comrades fall at every step of the way—AOCS, AI, primary, intermediate strike, advanced strike—so that completing the training and receiving wings genuinely deserves to be thought of as a lifetime achievement.

And yet the greatest rewards lie ahead. They include flying with a stick and throttle in airplanes that go fast, taking Gs and maneuvering crisply in any attitude, and having exclusive responsibility for an airplane worth millions of dollars. Above all, there is the profound self-satisfaction that comes with landing ten tons of jet aircraft onto a 600-foot carrier deck. Too, our naval aviator must be ready not just to fly but to fight, or at least to maintain such a high state of readiness that no actual fighting will ever be necessary.

Landing signal officers (LSOs) who will guide students to a landing gather on the deck of the training carrier USS Lexington *(AVT–16). Peter B. Mersky*

During carrier qualifications, or CQ, Skyhawks prepare to launch from USS John F. Kennedy *(CV–67). Peter B. Mersky*

The Navy training detachment's flight line at El Centro, California. The Training Command sends advanced students to the Imperial Valley for preliminary weapons training. Peter B. Mersky

TA–4J Skyhawk advanced trainers begin their takeoff roll at El Centro. Peter B. Mersky

Chapter 9

To the Fleet

Getting towards his mid-forties now, he's in superb shape and can still run five miles or wring out the most advanced jet fighter at the edge of the envelope. But, like many of us, if pressed, he'll admit that more flying years lie behind than ahead.

The commodore at Beeville feels that he has the best job in the Navy, running a training air wing with three squadrons which make jet pilots. He enjoys spending his time around the superbly capable young Americans who are struggling under pressure to become naval aviators. The commodore—protocol title for this senior Navy captain—is mature now and a little gray at the temples, and his only regret about his career as a naval aviator is that he can't go out and start all over again at the beginning.

"I'd trade places with any of you," he says.

He has gathered two dozen student naval aviators in his conference room at 10 a.m. to go over the "winging" ceremony scheduled for them at 3 p.m. this afternoon. It doesn't say in any rule book that he ought to meet with students about to receive their wings; it's just good sense. His routine is probably little different from that of a captain who came before him, will follow him or has a similar slot at another station.

He goes around the table double-checking names so he won't make a gaffe when introduced to a newly-winged aviator's girlfriend or grandmother ("How do you pronounce Poposki?"). He asks for impressions of the instructors and the training syllabus, promising *this* time at least, not to gig anybody for speaking out candidly. He invites students to criticize anything that happened in their entire eighteen months from AOCS

to golden wings—and nobody says anything. Making the transition from student to full-fledged officer and aviator requires a change of mindset and the change is still taking place.

He tells the soon-to-be aviators that even with wings of gold, they can't go it alone. "If your family doesn't like you flying for the Navy, you need to do something else."

Like any senior officer envious of the young people gathered to hear his wisdom, the commodore rambles a little about his own Navy career. His first tour was in F-8 Crusaders in Vietnam. They were single-seaters armed with cannons and they went forth to kill MiGs. That was in 1966-67, the height of the first campaign against North Vietnam. The squadron was caught up in cyclic operations around the clock, launching from the carrier to take on Hanoi's pitched defenses, day and night. A close friend was killed. Another was captured.

Returning home to a country not enamored then of men in uniform, he faced hard decisions. Should he stay in or try the more lucrative route with the airlines? He stayed. For one two-year period, his job consisted of ferrying F-8s to Hawaii, a five and one-half hour trip. Later, he flew F-4 Phantoms and F-14 Tomcats. "My wife and family supported me every inch of the way. I've never regretted staying in the Navy."

The "winging" ceremony is held at the club. To most recipients, the award of these wings will be among the half-dozen or so most treasured memories of a lifetime, right up there with marriage and the

Naval aviators and NFOs who fly from land make a vital contribution to national security but when much of the world thinks of the US Navy it thinks of the world's only large fleet of aircraft carriers. The aviator or NFO who serves in a carrier air wing must spend five to seven months at a time away from home and must regularly carry out flying duties which are, even with the best training in the world, dangerous. This look at the unique world of carrier aviation by an SH–3D Sea King pilot shows USS Independence *(CV–62) under steam. USN*

birth of a child. The ceremony has double meaning for those in the Navcad program who, until today, were not yet officers. They receive commission and wings together.

Wives, parents, relatives and friends gather to see the coveted wings of gold pinned on the Navy uniforms.

Nicknames

Naval aviators inescapably pick up nicknames—"handles" or "tactical callsigns"—which are the real-life equivalent of *Top Gun*'s Maverick and Goose. And yes, it makes sense for a flier to have a handle like Iron Belly, Fitz, Lucky, Horseshoes or Headbone. Or like Rat Breath, Puke, Sluggo, Deadeye and Pumpkin. When you're in a high-speed maneuver dodging enemy gun-fire and mixing it up with MiGs, you haven't got time to address your wingman as "Lieutenant junior grade Fitzsimmons" or even with a radio callsign like

"Panther three oh six." There isn't time. You say, "Fitz, break right!"

A naval aviator of NFO usually doesn't have much luck trying to decide what his own handle should be and, as much as he might want to be called Thunder-hawk or Lance he'll probably be stuck with what he gets. The student who ejected from a T–2C safely only to break his leg climbing down from a tree never had any choice about being nicknamed Trees. An ex-stockbroker for an investment firm calling itself bullish on America became, with no choice in the matter, Bull. NFO Joe Fives told a pal about having two pet dogs at home and became Two Dogs.

Fleet replenishment squadron

For those who'll operate from carriers, the next step after becoming a naval aviator or NFO is the fleet replenishment squadron (FRS). Formerly called a replacement air group (RAG) and still called a "rag" in jargon, this is the squadron which prepares you to go to sea in the aircraft you'll fly operationally. F–14 Tomcat squadrons are at Oceana, Virginia (for the Atlantic Fleet), and Miramar, California (for the Pacific); F–18 squadrons are at Cecil Field, Florida, and Lemoore, California, and so on. In the FRS, you not only learn your particular aircraft, you also learn how to land on a carrier in bad weather, at night.

In some ways, going through the FRS squadron is a little like beginning another phase of training. Says a newly assigned F–14 pilot, "You go through the FAM stage, which gets you familiarized with the jet and gets you flying it. Where these are single stick, the guy in back is your instructor on a FAM hop, but he can't fly the plane. He can just talk you through what you need to do. Then we have a basic weapons phase and that's just deploying your weapons the F–14 can carry. Then we have guns and that gets you used to firing the guns on the plane. And after that you learn tactics, including ACM [air combat maneuvering]."

Just keeping track of the FRS squadrons for the Atlantic and Pacific Fleets is a daunting task for an archivist, although the squadrons do not change often and are well settled in their identities. Aviators who went through the multi-engine pipeline and NFOs from the interservice undergraduate navigator training (IUNT) will join the P–3 Orion with VP–30 at Jacksonville, Florida, or VP–31 at Moffett Field, California. The latter will become the first FRS squadron for the future Lockheed P–7 patrol aircraft. Other aviators and NFOs with the same training will go to the Air Force for C–130 training at Little Rock, Arkansas, or to a private contractor for training in the Boeing E–6 long-range communications aircraft.

Naval aviators who earned their wings via the rotary wing pipeline will join the Sikorsky SH-3 Sea King with HS-1 at Jacksonville, Florida, or HC-1 at North Island, California; the Sikorsky SH-60F Seahawk antisubmarine helicopter with HS-10 at North Island; the Boeing H-46 Sea Knight with HC-3 at

Since this photo was taken, the Northrop F-5E Tiger has been replaced by the General Dynamics F-16N Fighting Falcon. Still, this interesting formation shows the major types of fixed-wing naval aircraft which Training Command graduates will fly—E-2C, F-14A, F-5E and TA-4J. USN

North Island; the Sikorsky H-53 Stallion with HM-12 at Norfolk, Virginia; the Sikorsky SH-60B LAMPS shipboard helicopter with HSL-40 at Mayport, Florida; the Kaman SH-2 Seasprite with HSL-30 at Norfolk or HSL-31 at North Island; or the Bell UH-1 Huey with HC-16 at Pensacola.

VT-4 at Pensacola has the sole mission of training Grumman E-2 Hawkeye/C-2 Greyhound crews in

Aircraft flown by Marine graduates of the jet strike syllabus include the RF-4B Phantom, F-18 Hornet, A-4M Skyhawk, and AV-8B Harrier II. The RE-4B was the last version of the Phantom to be operational and the A-4M remains active with Marine Reserve units. McDonnell Douglas

carrier qualifications. In all of these units, the object is the same—to get the new pilot or NFO up to speed in the aircraft to be flown during a naval career.

Our naval aviators and naval flight officers have made a remarkable transition during the long and difficult months on the path to wings of gold. From being a civilian, excited about aviation to be sure but still a little awkward of manner and new to the Navy's world, they have gone to flying with the Fleet and serving as officers. They stand up straighter, lead others, fly and are ready finally to serve aboard a carrier or at a naval air station—flying that Tomcat, Orion or Stallion for a living.

There are plenty of other people who would willingly trade places for that opportunity. It really is a special world, reserved solely for the best of the best.

In The Pipeline

By ENS Mark Hutchins

ENS Hutchins has been reporting on his progress in the pursuit of Navy wings since the Winter 1988 issue of Wings of Gold.

What better way to finish up the training command syllabus than flying four ACM—air combat maneuvering—hops in the TA-4J *Skyhawk?* That's real excitement and makes me appreciate "the good deals" available to today's Naval Aviators.

The last sortie signalled the end of my tour in the training command and meant that I would finally get my wings as a Naval Flight Officer. It was a wonderful feeling after that final flight when my instructor presented me with leather wings which I now wear proudly on my flight suit. Later, my wife, Cindy, pinned on my gold wings at VT-86 graduation ceremonies, an exciting and memorable day. Some of my fellow "wingees" pounded the wings into my chest as part of the celebration.

I feel most fortunate to get my first choice in aircraft and location. I have been assigned to VA-42, the A-6 FRS (fleet replacement squadron) at NAS Oceana, Virginia, to fly as a BN (bombardier/navigator) in the A-6E *Intruder.* Receiving these orders was as exhilarating as winning the wings. I have wanted to join the *Intruder* community from the beginning of my interest in Naval Aviation.

In reviewing the year and four months, I realize more than ever how great is the distance between that first day of AI (aviation indoctrination) in November 1988 and graduation. I studied and flew in the T-34C *Mentor,* the T-2 *Buckeye,* the T-47 Cessna *Citation,* and the TA-4J *Skyhawk.* I learned a lot in each, commencing with book and manual study, progressing into flight simulators, and then getting into the real cockpit. The dos and don'ts, and responsibilities of an NFO, were hammered carefully and thoroughly into us.

I know that I have only mastered but a small part of what I must master to become a fleet BN. In perspective, it seems that the training command is really a place to prove yourself capable of handling what is ahead, rather than learning all there is to know. As to the even greater challenges of the future, I feel I am ready for them.

I have a whole new aircraft to study and learn, not to mention weapons systems that don't exist in the training command.

You never know enough in this business. But the training command taught me the basics and gave me a foundation of knowledge upon which to build.

I am extremely proud of my wings and what they stand for. I have worked hard and long for them and will do my best to measure up to the duties I must face as an A-6 *Intruder* bombardier navigator in the fleet.

First printed in Wings of Gold, *Summer 1990*

Afterword & Acknowledgments

The training of naval aviators and naval flight officers is an intricate and dynamic process which is changing every day. To cite but one example, when this volume went to press the T-45 Goshawk trainer system was still some time away from entering service; its role in training will not be fully clear until the mid-1990s.

Most of the impressions in *Wings of Gold* will remain accurate through the end of the century but nothing which appears here should be taken as official or inevitable. While generous assistance was received from the Navy, this volume is the work of authors, editors and publishers, and should not be viewed as having the endorsement of the Navy or the Department of Defense. Mistakes appearing in the text are solely the fault of the authors.

It must be added, however, that a work of this nature, especially on a subject so complex, would be impossible without the help of many who contributed their time and effort.

Peter B. Mersky was extremely generous with his time and counsel; he helped us to fill many blanks and improved this work in almost every respect.

Some of the language in this volume is adapted with permission from US Navy publications; we especially want to thank LCDR Rick Burgess, editor of *Naval Aviation News*, and LCDR Dave Parsons, former editor of *Approach*.

For permission to reprint the "In the Pipeline" articles we thank the Association of Naval Aviation and, in particular, the author LTJG Mark Hutchins, and *Wings of Gold* editor Rosario (Zip) Rausa and executive director CAPT Frederick J. Orrick.

We also want to acknowledge the generous help of those listed below.

At Beeville: CAPT William P. Bertsch, LCDR Sandy Jones, CDR Pat Doyle and LT Chad Hill

At Corpus Christi: 2LT Paul Gomez, ENS Laine Konrad and ENS Ann McGlauflin

At Kingsville: CAPT Lonny K. McClung, CDR Chuck Giger, 2LT Marshall Denney, ENS Jeanine M. Stanton and ENS Rebecca Colonna

At Meridian: ENS James Grunwald and ENS James Riddle

At Pensacola: Kay Estey and Harry White

At Whiting field: LTJG Beth Murray and YN3 Audrey Anderson

With the Fleet: Jeff Cartwright, ENS Joe Merrell, LT Joseph R. Fives, LT Greg Smith and LT Jim Wood

Among the fraternity: Jim Benson, George R. Cockle, Harry Gann, R. J. Mills, Jr., Al Mongeon, Dorsie Page, Norman Polmar, The Gang at Roy's and Douglas A. Zalud

And a special thanks to Rose DiFilippo of Canon USA, Inc. for graciously providing Ketchell with camera equipment.